Last Stanza
Poetry Journal

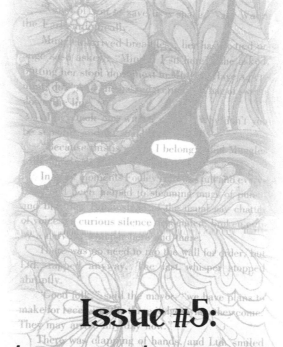

Issue #5:
Lost / Found / Rediscovered

Edited by Jenny Kalahar

Heather A. Smith Blaha, artist

Stackfreed
Press

Welcome to the fifth issue, a celebration and lamentation of things and people and places lost, found, and rediscovered. Poets were invited to write on this theme and to submit photos that are now collected in an album on Last Stanza Poetry Association's Facebook page. A secondary interpretation of the theme was to submit poems written long ago that were never published elsewhere but that the poets still love and want to see revived in print.

The artist for Issue #5 is Heather A. Smith Blaha. She, too, is a revivalist. Heather uses discarded books to create sharp, emotional, and startling blackout poetry by painting and/or drawing around those words that are a part of her poem. Check out her full color artworks online.

Thank you, poets.
Thank you, readers.

Jenny Kalahar, editor

Look Homeward, Angel

after Thomas Wolfe

Although I'm told *you can't go home again,*
the logic failed at the sound of a crow's rasping caw

echoing through a portal of leafless tress pressed
against the leaden sky of a winter morning,

swallowing lost time, summoning things past,
and once again I am walking at dawn

from a pasture to the milking barn, feeling
the crunch of frozen grass at footfall,

hearing the pulse of machines steady as a heartbeat,
the clangor of metal chutes opening and closing

as Holsteins bump in and out of order,
barely overcoming their inertia while they

stare obliviously with pure black eyes so large
they hold my reflection, a reflection that says

look homeward, angel,

the sentiment too genuine for mere theory,
and summoning cellular memory

of retreats into the solitude of the barn loft,
and the fragrance of alfalfa hay and sight

of its dust floating in a shaft of slanted light
shining through chinks in the side of the barn,

and I reach to touch one more time
the burnished handle of a hay hook

hanging on a wall with a tangle of binder-twine,
thin coarse slack-twists of sisal someone

thought to save as probably useful,
then forgot.

James Green

Small Neighborhood

The new puppy is afraid of cars,
so when McSwain's black pick-up rounds the turn,
I make sure she's in the grass so she won't choke
herself pulling back. Every day he waves at me,
leaning down for a closer look like he wants to be
my friend. Now's his chance. We've both
been through the flood together, from across
the acre where his house, built on a polished rise
of rock, tiptoed above the brown water. Mine waded.
If we were talkative people, we'd have a lot to say.

Turns out, we aren't. Looks like we wish we didn't
have to speak at all. It's so formal when it whispers out,
how are you today and *fine thanks* and *very well.*
Nothing about the days our house steamed ankle-deep
in sludge, his circled by a moat, and nobody went
anywhere, especially him, once I found a guy with a boat
who paddled me down to rescue our dogs
and frantic cat the cops were afraid to touch
when they collected us. What's the matter with all
of us? So much trouble for so few people, lost

and uncertain across short distances. Maybe
I hoped for nothing, or maybe I hoped our neighbors
thought us human—that mattered when we lost
our earnings in peace and quiet. Like a friend said,
Lesbians in Oklahoma, though. We just don't know
what the folks next door are saying where we never go,
which covers pretty much anywhere they might show,
since mostly Oklahoma neighbors spend time in church.
When they're ill, the congregation appears with dishes.
That means we're on the edge and very sure of it.

My neighbor's white house is new and twice as big
as mine. At night when I walk the puppy, moonlight

shines on his metal roof and reflects from mine.
I don't see much else. He's over there, he and his wife
and irritable teenage son, and that's all I need to know.
The swimming pool. The locked gates. When he bent
and waved through the windshield like he was my friend,
I laughed a little. I couldn't understand—we hadn't even
spoken. But this makes sense. Knowing and not caring, and
only sometimes having to speak and getting it over with.

Lisa Lewis

How it Worked

You crawled out through the quarter-size door,
groaning like a bear as you rose, unshaven,
the other stockpiled seasons left behind in the dark.

A year's dust blown from the snug blue box,
its *Universal* brand embossed on top,
then down to the kitchen's sunny clatter

where you took it apart like a gun, sloshing
each silvered piece in soapy water: auger shaft
pulled from squat body with its C-clamp legs,

blonde wooden grip spinning on the crank,
clover-shaped cutter, slippery in the suds.
Directions left folded, yellowing even then,

as the bird seared and spat and spuds
lurked like pale rocks under a scum of foam.
Beside them, the giblets simmered and bobbed,

adding their blood-smell to the soupy air:
tender liver and kidneys, gizzard's fatty riddle,
the soft rubber heart. Hardly enough to warrant

the grinder's steel weight, but that's how it worked—
each piece of inner life dropped in the maw
to emerge beneath, parallel worms of crumbly meat

you added like salt to our dressing and gravy
each November, each time around, back when
we believed one month must lead to the next.

Here, you want to give it a couple of turns?
Now when I see one at a garage sale, shining
on the half-shell in its sturdy case, it's your

ghost hand that reaches to touch flaky plating,
worn handle, or the generous nubbled ring
that spins so easily into place in a gone world.

Scott Lowery

All-Ireland

He looks the youngest one up there on stage,
like he might still go home to his mum for meals
instead of this journeywork trade in jigs and reels
with a matter-of-fact deadpan to mask his age.
In turn, he's introduced by one of his chums—
four times All-Ireland on whistle—but set
after set, he only strums guitar, not ready yet
to step up front.
    There should be a roll of drums
when he seems to spot the flute beneath his chair
as if he's discovered quite an interesting stick,
then lifts it to his lips, blood kindling his cheeks,
and off we go! aloft on the eloquent air
to a village land of river, stone, and brick,
where a boy might often sing before he speaks.

Scott Lowery

Anniversary Card with Birds

Looking back that far, like a twenty-something
    trying to call up infant scenery:
        no words to name what's there.

Were we babies? There was a sense I had of you,
    a stranger but known, as a bird knows
        to dart among spring multitudes until

drawn face-to-face with its own kind.
    How could we know? There was a leap
        somewhere early, into fear, into bed:

bodies as well as eyes squeezed tight
    then open, little by little, to light.
        In the old curricula: food, nests,

what we took from need and habit,
    none of it sudden except the deaths
        life yanks away, the rest all measured

and made from scratch. In each history
    its battles, each philosophy its skeptics.
        This path not brightly burning: doubt

always buzzing darkly in these woods.
    Still, standing at our front window,
        moon full, you asleep, I blindly know

how it all comes around. Under cold sheets
    your warm legs complete the sentence
        I was saying, and it's gone. No matter—

I remember this: whichever branch I grab
    for singing, then pause a bit to listen, I hear
        your voice return, and matched to mine.

Scott Lowery

7

Goodbye Kiss

A kiss flares up from fear
or expectations of loss.
Don't leave, it pleads,
already in mourning as

the farewell descends
like a bell jar.
The avid kiss wavers,
the heart withdraws. Soon

there'll be nothing but words
like sparks blown from an ember,
flickering in a wire that stretches
from a number to a number.

Joseph Hutchison

The Hands in Sleep

let go of your wrists
and crawl off into an ocean

therefore the vertigo
in your sudden
reach to kill the clock's alarm
the prickling in your fingers
like spirits called up
at a séance

therefore too
those skull-pounding
tidal rumblings as you wake
with your shaken sense
of having traveled deeply
through the dark

and touched
others of our kind

Joseph Hutchison

Valley Morning

Snow crystals twinkling in morning wind,
mind alive to the light and that glacial peak

standing forth into it. Higher still, a cloud,
and a cloud, and a cloud. And the valley feels

full of ghosts: pale ones in yellow canvas pants,
or in checkered gingham and cobbled shoes,

darker ones in beaded deerskin moccasins,
in elk-hide dresses embroidered and fringed.

Like you, they all turned to this mountain,
and dreamed, and believed. Strange: how any

moment can deepen into years, even centuries;
how easily we can vanish into the images—

melting into time like a glint of snow

Joseph Hutchison

Instead, I worried the bottom of my long skirt would get caught in the brambles on the trail. For steeper and narrower the ... we got to our campsite. The rest of the children would be gathering wood to get us through the coming winter. Cousin Eliza had just reminded me about how we lost little Jack during the coldest months last year. He caught a chill and just never recovered. Everyone was waiting for us to return with the mail. A package had come from the Sears Roebuck Company.

"Olden Day, Eliza could hardly contain her excitement. "I can't wait to find out what's inside," she said.

"Well, be careful. Don't shake it. It might break."

"It's too heavy to break." Eliza frowned and then, from inside my backpack my cell phone buzzed.

Or it was the other way around, but either way it took ... that was going on. It would ... as when you're in a really good book and you forget you are read-ing at all ... a voice, the sound of the television ... feels like an ... The way you can fall in a dream and wake up in your own bed, wondering which is more real.

Michael.

It must be.

Everything fell away, the long dresses and high button boots, the package wrapped in brown paper, even the memories of little Jack and long, cold winters. The trail was narrow, and I let my

Lost, In A Dream

Generally, Vincent's dreams are pleasant ones,
and he is thankful for that. Yes, in many of them,
he is lost in an unknown city and increasingly worried
he will not be able to get where he is going, but then he wakes
and visits the bathroom simply to urinate, which
was evidently what the pressure in the dream was all about.
Relieved, he returns to bed and sleeps soundly until dawn.
Vincent finds those dreams a bit comic.

But last night's was different. He had gone to bed
feeling lonely, old, and anxious. Melatonin, however,
eased him on his way, making him feel okay—although he missed
his sister. (Nan, who had been one year older than he,
had died eight years ago.)
Now the dream spoke to Vincent. Usually, his dreams

were silent. He saw words in them, but the words were seldom
vocal. These were. Only two—but distinctly pronounced
so there could be no doubt as to what they said,
and at the right volume for Vincent,
who takes his hearing aids out before he goes to bed.
"She's dead," they announced—just that, as though meant
to be an example, in a class for non-native speakers, of what
finality means with no questions to ask of the dream teacher.

Jonathan Bracker

Becky Gives a Middle School Class Report

First, there is The State of Loneliness:
In Loneliness, many people want someone
to be with them, a lot.
There, almost everyone is almost always getting ready
to go over to the nearest occupied park bench
in order to nervously smile and say, "May I sit down?"

Second, there is The State of Aloneness:
In Aloneness, most of its few citizens, when approached
in public or at home, mutter, "Oh, it's you again!
I thought I was free of your presence."
There, folks attempt to buddy up
only with their warring selves.
This takes a good deal of their time.
(If they go to town, they sometimes sit atop wooden park tables
in one of the still-gracious public parks, looking out
with wonder.)

And thirdly, she says, there is The State of Onliness.
According to *Webster's Revised Unabridged,*
1913 edition, "Onliness" is "the quality
or state of being the only one of an indicated
or implied kind or category."
Little is known, as yet, about this one.

And then Becky ducks her head, and she sits down.

                                        Jonathan Bracker

The Emergence of Anti-Heroes
Amid the Sudden Erosion of the Western Canon

After you scratch your nose, Sherlock Holmes disappears from the literary canon while you return to your coffeehouse table with a cappuccino. Doyle never wrote *The Hound of the Baskervilles*. No more of Dr. Moriarty's schemes. The authenticity of "Elementary, my dear Watson" now moot. You scan the cafe. No one seems bothered by the onset of your superpower except for the coed in the corner. The one who was reading Louise Penny when you arrived. Still the trembling lips and panic in her eyes could be a passing infatuation. You brush your nose once more, erasing Elvis Presley. "Hound Dog." "Heartbreak Hotel." That Flying Elvii movie with Nicolas Cage and Kirk Russell, just a figment of your suspicious mind. The madness spreads through your central nervous system the way it must have propagated during Caligula's reign when the emperor mistook himself for a god. Background music hisses from a transistor radio somewhere behind the counter—a dirge with violins and an out-of-tune piano. You wonder whether you've gone too far. Back in the days of synthesizers and syncopated baselines, the bouncers at King's Corner called you "Tony Manero." You lived for disco. "Jive Talkin'" and "Stayin' Alive." But you've rubbed out Barry Gibb along with Evelyn Wood and Katie Couric. The girl in the corner sobs into her mug. A grey-haired gentleman tears blank pages from what once was a Vincent Price biography. Crams them into a trash can. Behind the counter, the manager waltzes to a baroque cantata with the red-headed barista you fancy. You become more deliberate. Ed Wood crosses your mind until you scald your hands with the boiled sludge you've been drinking. Until you surrender to your obsession and evaporate Ayn Rand. The barista eyes you with that look substitute teachers practice at their orientations. She glances at the grieving patrons and tugs at her right ear.

Michael Brockley

Gorilla Monsoons Jr. Bellies Up to the Bar for a Tequila Sunrise at the Bald-Headed Sax Player's Lounge

I spend too many evenings spinning on a barstool at Baldy's. Nobody plays the devil's horn here. But you can find the Left Bower and the False Hood lying about their professional wrestling careers at the only round table in the joint. That's where they make me the butt of all their jokes, remind me I lost every match. *But myself I can't deceive.* The False Hood spins balderdash about the Bat collapsing on top of me after a play-by-play buffoon cold-cocked me with a frying pan to the skull bone. Leftie chuckles through his madcap replay of how Bobo Brazil's son tossed me out of the ring in an unsanctioned bout in Bruiserville. But the bill collectors don't send their repo notices to this neighborhood, and Baldy keeps a double-stacked Wurlitzer tucked under an autographed black-and-white of Conway Twitty. We've worn out three 45s of "It's Only Make Believe" by pressing E6 on the juke. *My heart I can't control. You rule my very soul.* Whenever the Born Loser stumbles in, we gather around for his latest boasts of being Joe Athlete Stud Supreme. He replays that night at IU where he shut down Larry Legend in a pickup game and dribbled coast to coast against the French Lick hick to finish with a Godzilla Jam. Claims cameos on *Seinfeld.* An on-again, off-again with what's her name from *Friends.* And all the while the False Hood hoots like a loon when he smells Loser's cock-and-bull. All year Baldy keeps a sign-up sheet posted beside the dart board for our annual junket to Tribute Band Lalapalooza. This year the WWE pretenders half-nelsoned me into singing "Keep Your Hands to Yourself." With threats of Crypt Keeper sleeper-holds if I weasel out. We keep all the Gus Macker Toilet Bowl trophies on a shelf beside Baldy's home-brewed beer display from the days when we skipped the pick and made the most of a flat-footed roll. *You are my every dream but it's only make believe.* After last call, we return home to women who have loved us for more years than we deserve.

Michael Brockley

Personality Survey of the Toes of My Left Foot

The first is the biggest piggie,
who obviously hogged all the milk,
goes to market or wherever else
he damned well pleases. A clod, a brawler,
he's the one who gets bloodied.

The second is an aristocrat,
longer than Stubb, to his right,
and more slender.
He would prefer to stay home
and avoid the vulgar.

The third is a useful, solid
citizen, middle-of-the-road,
can be counted on,
pays his taxes, eats
roast beef.

The fourth feels cheated,
lives too far from the center
of power, gets stepped on,
goes hungry.

The fifth isn't wanted
and knows it, his mom and dad
got drunk that night, and careless.
An after-thought, a tailgate,
a surprise, he cries *we all count!*
We are in it together—we, *not* I:
we we we we we.

James Bowden

Matryoshkas

There never was a female colossal silly on the level of Kant or Hegel. – WH Auden

Enigmas nesting, one in the other,
each daughter in her mother, her mother,
her mother, stacked, all the way back to Eve
(or Lucy?), clothed since one cannot deleave
figs and reenter the Garden thereby.

The spawn all smile alike, as sinners bent,
sharing her guilt. Men have no equivalent,
are dead ends, appendages, left to hang
out, don't stack up: as Nicodemus sang,
how can one possibly be born again?

Once males have left the nest, they feel the loss
(wrote John Fowles of men*), their status slag, dross;
hence the dolls are always female, and red
most often (*women are best at detail, said
Fowles). Male offshoots are often surly—

spent cartridges, empty casings, cordite.
Then—just once!—pigments changed to purest white
(by Design or DNA?), her humble
heart pierced, her Byzantine life a jumble
of wise men, wine-tasting, and crowds, crowds, crowds.

Her sorrow was such as felt by no man:
there *is* no sound like that of a woman
who has lost her child. First horror, spasms
of black noonday sun, the deepest chasms
open. And will not close. They will not close.

Until the grave's womb is riven, opened
to joy in the morning, gloom upended,
with each maid sweetly smiling—one of us!
One of us! The riddle unravels thus,
and men learn what the women always knew.

James Bowden

17

Storm and the Tree

The storm that split the tree was not severe,
but the oak was old, been there all my life,
and many lives before, shading much strife,
and woe, and happiness. It was there.
It was a fixture. Expected, landmark
that now is riven; halved that which was whole.
And hollow. A shock—nothing left. No bole,
yet it had stood leaved so long. Now with bark
peeled, it's trashy, awaiting removal.
And it will be moved, with dozer, shovel.
It will be sawn and chipped, dragged off in iron chains.
Such is life, such is death. Now for a change
of scene: young Freud, at an opening
of a new corpse, heard his senior opine,
"Such arteries! Of course he could not live!"
To which said Sigmund, "Yet he did survive
until yesterday." Quite well said, doctor.
Soon I shall put my affairs in order.

James Bowden

Giraffe

Head in the acacias,
the giraffe eats
its way toward me.
Its long neck moves
as a model moves
down this runway
of no applause.

A distant growl,
lions in the grass.
The giraffe lopes
away. Legs, neck,
head disappear.
The moon a giraffe
in the night sky.

Peter Huggins

Peony Resurrected

The razed peony bush
resprouted—unlikely growth
from cruelly (unnecessarily) lopped

stems and leaves after last April's flowering. I'd
glared from my bedroom window
at the grounds maintenance guy, an ominous
giant hovering over that peony bush, begging

him to spare that unnecessary
cruelty. When I dared to
glance again, that peony bush had
vanished. But now, as spring

deepens into wilder green and deer
multiply among the brush, ants
swarm around hard green peony buds,
eager for the crack of
sweetness and pungence after
stormwash.

Hiromi Yoshida

gray eyes sparkled. None of her stress-zits showed. Half in shadow, she was beautiful, perfectly fitted, maybe even the tiniest bit suave. She watched a little fantasy in her mind: *Lori walks into the airport with an air of confidence, striding as casually as if she'd been flying all her life. The crowd parts to make way for her. Everyone is in awe of her beauty, her* je ne sais quoi. *Then someone steps forward. It is an incredibly handsome man—TV-star handsome, movie star handsome, better looking than any guy in all of Pickford County. His fingers brush Lori's arm, and the mere touch sends a thrill through her body.* (Did that ever really happen outside of romance novels? Lori decided it could.)

"Excuse me," he whispers. "I am a fashion designer. I must know—where did you get that incredible creation. That gold dress?" In her fantasy, Lori is humble as well as gorgeous. *"I made it. It's a Butterick pattern."*

"Ah, but you have transformed it," the man says. "You have given it swell and beauty. Will you—"

And then Lori was done. Did she really want this fantasy man admiring her sewing skills? She didn't even like to sew that much. And what was he going to offer her? A job? Not very romantic. A date? Come on, how old would this fantasy man have to be to be a successful fashion designer? She was only fourteen. It was kind of gross if he was too much older than that.

This was a problem Lori often had with fantasies. After a certain point, they just weren't very practical.

Time

Where does Time tick away to?
The days. The hours. Each minute
seemingly passes both slowly and swiftly into night.
Darkness clings to me,
softly sings to me. It brings truths hidden
within once-recognizable fragments of existence in
this collective reality. My reality. Yours. Woven
together in the awakened world.

Where am I now? Do you remember how we shivered
in the dark—alone, quiet, smart—
how light made no difference at all?

Yet here.
There. Resilience overrides the fear.
That is all I see. All I hear.

And our heroes never did any wrong.
Never sung any unpleasant songs. Never
waved goodbye in the late-day sunlight.
Never died by the roadside. Never disappeared
into the days. Hours. Minutes.

And when we awoke, birds
still flew. Everyone we knew
stayed the same, came in from the rain,
and warmed their hands
over the fire.

James Eric Watkins

The Way Smoke Moves

Smoke transforms
from something to nothing to everything,
much like a spirit returns to the universe
after it has lived all the lives it can live,
rolling continuously through the changes.

It bends and flips and twists,
spirals and spins, streaks, streams,
unfurls from its source,
gathers in clouds,
hovers and whispers

Secrets

As a soul would.
As only a soul would speak.
Without words. Without sound.
Without explanation, shape,
or destination. Simply a calming
clarification. Communicating:
a reflection of inner self,
of how everything and everyone
are interwoven and connected

and simply too uninhibited
to be contained
by something as insignificant
as physical form.

James Eric Watkins

There's a Shift in the Universe

So of course it begins again,
those dark alluring vibrations
awakening in me fragments from
a past half-buried with the heady scent

of a lost weekend in San Francisco
in the hidden nook, pathetically
spurning mere friendly connection to
keep your torrential rage at bay. Pity —

Hotel Mirabelle is no more. Dreams
(once a vivid myriad of possibilities)
seem to hover coldly just out of reach,
and some doors will remain closed.

Spellbound, I sink into familiar yet odd
retrograde patterns coursing through tidal
veins, seeking only the whispered solace
in the midst of chaos.

Melody Wang

losing myself in

hours of isolation and the same wistful tunes
looping on lonely evening walks, failing to notice

burnt-orange, magenta-striated skies as I
traipse from grey building to loveless dorm,

ivy-draped concrete looming, beckoning,
so far from the home I once knew, seeking

the solace of my mind, breathwork to
stave off anxiety's fog, unfamiliar shadows

elongating, a tinny ringing in my left ear
in places where people took their last breaths,

their quiet ghosts eager to follow me home
as the darkness grew longer still.

Perhaps they knew their stories
were still unfinished,

perhaps they knew
I would listen

Melody Wang

Mom at Ninety-nine

My mother-in-law loses things day by day:
touch, vision, taste, blood, hearing, sense of smell.
Only shadows, vague odors, and blandness remain.
She stores herself in anecdotes rehearsed over time
of little injuries and triumphs as teacher and mother.
She hasn't lost her mind.

She loses her place, her stockings, her tapes,
contact lens, her balance, her hair, and weight.
She hasn't lost her pride.

She's lost energy, earphones,
teeth, friends, the ballast of her bosom.
But she hasn't lost her spine.

Mornings, she gathers what remains and
walks upstairs to the kitchen,
then drinks hot water straight.
Rigid fingers scan pillboxes
for the right day, the right time.
She shares half an apple with the dog.
Side by side, they hear the news on NPR.
She showers and puts on freshly washed clothes,
applies powder, lipstick and dons a wig.
At these prices, kid, we call it a hairpiece.
She hasn't lost her flair.

For lunch, she slices a tomato and pours on salt,
eats the other half of apple and a bit of bread.
Folds laundry, pressing out wrinkles with wrinkled hands,
dries dishes and stacks them on the counter.
All afternoon, she reads books on tape,
smiles at Jane Austen and frowns on Jane Smiley,
answers the phone, and recites my calls when I get home.
Later, she quizzes me, "Did you call Leslie?"

Evenings, we watch *Sex and the City*
until she walks out halfway through.
Good night, kids, I'll listen to my tapes and leave the slapstick to you.

Day and night, the button on her watch calls out the time.
She has her pride, her spine, her flair. She has her mind.

Lois Baer Barr

Height

For my mother, Ethel Cooper Baer, 1924-2012

At her tallest, Mom was four foot, nine and a half.
You might think smoking stunted her growth,
but she came from a line of tiny women
who were breadwinners and who hated bullies.
Mom shook her fist at our neighbor Tom Johnson,
Semper Fi tattoo on his bicep, beer belly,
face red with anger at my brother and friends.
They'd silenced Frosty's song once more and stolen
Rudolph's nose. *Get off my porch. How dare you
come here with a gun?*

Her feet barely reached the pedals, but she stood tall
when she won piano contests as a girl.
Stood tall in her uniform as a student WAC.
A giant among autistic children who
learned to socialize to her songs and how to put
Kotex pads in their panties.

She played chamber music for soirées but slipped
in the shower before a party, braking four ribs.
Then life began to steal inches off her height,
moved them to her waist.

At four foot eight, despite pain, she accompanied
a klezmer group, Volterin gel pack on her back.
Donned earphones to play scales on her electric
keyboard at night, Mozart concertos by day
on her baby grand.

At four foot seven, she chauffeured, cooked and cared
for Dad. *Isn't she pretty?* he repeated
and repeated and repeated. She never
believed it. She lost patience, lost sleep,
but whenever I phoned, she'd say *Hi honey!,*
her voice pecan brittle sweet.

When Dad lost his way delivering Meals on Wheels,
she became his GPS. He followed her
around the house, sat in the shade while she led
pool aerobics, her head just a bit above
the water.

Lost Dad at four foot five. From her recliner,
she worked crosswords puzzles and cross-stitched quilts
for all her grandkids, solved hidden phrases
on *Wheel of Fortune.*

At four foot four, her elbow was crushed like
a pack of Saltines. Her spirit shattered too.
No more Mozart.

Lying in the ICU, she let her step-grandson
come in when I tried to keep him out. I was
angry he hadn't visited her in months.
Honey, he's nineteen. He would live with the guilt,
and I'm going to die.

Lois Baer Barr

Kansas, Old Abandoned House

House, weathered, bathed in grays,
appears lonely tonight on a Kansas prairie.
The human theater once lived inside is gone now,
buried in the back, along a dark trail
behind that outhouse.
Old woodchipper in the shed, rustic, worn,
no gas, no thunder, no sound.
Remember the old coal bin, now open to the wind,
but no one left to shovel the coal.
Pumpkin patches, corn mazes, hayrides—all gone.
Deserted ghostly boys and girls
still swing abandoned in the prairie wind.
Unheated rooms no longer have children
to fret about. Cheerleaders long gone,
the banal house chills once again. It is winter.
Three lone skinny crows perched out of sight on barren branches,
silhouetted in early morning hints of pink, those blues,
wait with hunger strikes
as snow settles beneath moonlit skies.
Kansas becomes a quiet place in those first snowfalls.
There is the dancing of crows,
lonely wind, creaking doors,
no oil in the joints.

Michael Lee Johnson

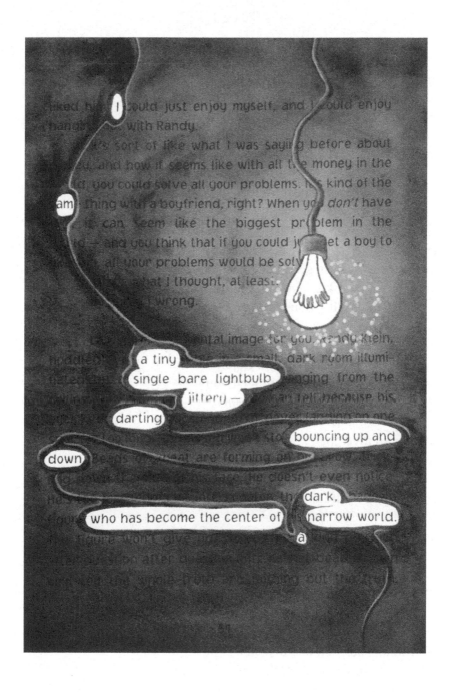

To the 628 Souls

of those children who have been separated
from parents and have no idea where
to find them, you are welcome to come
into our open house. We want to adopt

you all, as my wife and I adopted two
children some forty-one and thirty-eight
years ago from Bogotà, Colombia.
Don't worry, my children, we have

plenty of room in our livable house,
which stretches from sea to shining sea.
Come on into our kitchen, you big souls
of little children. It's bound to be raining

outdoors, but our roof has no leaks.
My wife will love to cook you Cajun
soul food. Some days we will feed you
with love, some days with love songs,

others with love poems. There's
a singer-songwriter who will sing
to keep you Forever Young, make
sure no Hard Rain falls on you,

and his light comes shining on each
of your 628 beautiful souls when you
come into our house. His Uncle Woody
will sing you his anthem, telling you this

land of our house is your land, this land
is our land, and each one of you is
welcome to stay in our country as
long as your hearts and souls may crave.

Norbert Krapf

Father Loss

I remember how glad we all were after
arriving home to be, sadly, together again.
We expressed our relief too vigorously,

so I shushed everyone as if someone
must take charge, and as the eldest,
hugged our mother, who was sobbing

with an ancient, primal grief.
She was wracked by the sudden
loss of the man who fathered us,

her children, and who was her mate
and companion for decades.
I neither had nor needed words.

Our bodies clung together
as only survivors can. Her
shaking grief grabbed hold of me

and carried me with her
as we rode together the bucking
waves of the dark waters of loss.

Norbert Krapf

Trixie

Trixie was a rat terrier who lived
in a small house our father built
just beyond the picnic table. Winters,

when snow and ice came to roost on her roof
we put straw on and in it for her to sleep on.
She pulled her chain inside and shivered,

but never resorted to low moan or high bark.
When a fierce storm left arctic winds howling
into the open door of her frozen house, we led

her down the basement steps into the cellar
where we had prepared a bed of straw. She
slept below shelves of canned green beans,

sweet and sour pickles, tomato and grape juice,
peaches, and crocks of grape and blackberry
wine sweet to the tongue. When we came

down the steps with warm water to lap and food
for her to eat, she rubbed her nose on our hands.
Her eyes said the sweetest four-letter word.

Norbert Krapf

My Brother and Schrödinger's Cat

When my brother died (perhaps now,
perhaps some time from now,
say, twelve or fifteen years hence),
I got to thinking. While we weren't close,
we shared a room. He taught me hockey
and jazz, the Brunswick label, Blue Note,
the off-beat, the flatted fifth, double-time,
Kook, Diz, Chet. Desmond's alto runs
through my life, it's Ariadne's thread.

His radio played from midnight on.
I'd awake to showers of notes flooding down
like starfall, listen awhile, fall back asleep.
When he played his clarinet, it squealed
as if being strangled. He'd put on a 78
and struggle to comp behind the soloist,
chasing him up and down the scale,
landing on the note every so often, the way,
in traffic, sometimes you see the same car.

His horn was weak, but his whistling
(he did a great rendition of *Salt Peanuts*)
would have won first chair in any band:
Kenton, Basie, Mingus, Duke. If only
they scored charts for a whistler.

I got to missing him, especially during
Stanley Cup finals, so I went to visit him
in Pasadena. He still whistles great.

Bruce Ducker

Dear Young Self

Thank you for not unmasking
until you had the tools to begin
that naked journey.

Although you did not emerge
unscathed, thank you
for protecting yourself enough
to swagger your way from
embellishment to something
resembling self-esteem.

When you could not elude
the vile demons and their fangs,
thank you for taking your inner self
away from it all, for separating
from your body and storing unfelt
memories in the plush silver
scrolled box lined with red velvet
in which you kept a many-faceted
crystal the size of a marble.

Oh, younger self, you darling
little survivor, I still have
our box and magic crystal,
a reminder of how,
through thwarted growth,
you side-eyed beauty, waiting
like the Mistress of the Future,
to deftly recompose
into who you have become,
into who we are yet becoming.

Debbi Brody

Lost Photograph

I have never seen this photograph. It still exists but will never be found.
The photo of my great-grandfather, Andrew, and his third wife, Matilda,
both of them seated in a wicker divan
                                        brought outside from the parlor.
The photo of his two children, Effie and Glenn, and her three children,
Roy, Marshall, and Ellen, these five arranged in stiff, detached poses
behind their parents.
                        They are all waiting, staring straight ahead, trying
not to move, because the exposure takes two minutes. Farther back
is the farmhouse, a mile south of Windfall, Indiana.
                                                        On the right,
the picket fence and the windmill. The strange monochromatic light
of the midwestern summer is all around them, and the incessant calling
of cicadas.
            Just visible, in the side yard, is the natural-gas flambeau
that was never extinguished, by night or by day. It is tear-shaped,
and burns pure white, like a flaw in the negative.
                                        I have seen this photo,
in my dreams, again and again. Sixty years later, my grandmother
described it for me, in considerable detail.
                        She remembered that it hung first in their parlor,
and then in someone else's parlor, and then gradually it disappeared,
was lost track of.
                    It was enclosed in a gilded ornamental frame
that cost five dollars. The photograph itself cost three dollars.
It was taken by an itinerant photographer, a red-headed Irishman
who stopped one day in his wagon, out at the main gate, and asked
if he could water his horse.
                            It is a photo that still exists, somewhere,
in some old shop or antique store, high up on a dusty shelf, kept
all this time because of the frame. It has been over a hundred years
since it was taken. It has been over a hundred years since anyone
wondered who these people were.
                                No one knows who is in the picture now.
No one recognizes the father in his beard, the woman with somber eyes,
the girls in their pinafores, the oldest boy in his borrowed frock coat.
Everything is sepia-toned, everything is flat, everything is forgotten.

> Yet the photo still exists somewhere.
> Every so often I remember it, and find myself reaching out in the hope
> of touching it, of putting my fingers up to that flame
> > never extinguished by night or by day.

Jared Carter

You, itinerant chapman, who went from farm
to farm carrying a cardboard suitcase full
of Hugo's novels in bad translations, the works
of Scott and Browning, George Eliot and Burns—

You, old drifter, whose faded advertisement
is still pasted in my grandfather's books—
those Victorian reprints on wood-chip paper,
signatures buckled, cheap bindings cracked—

Agents Wanted   Catalogue Free
Book Dealer   News Dealer
Chas. F. Howard Windfall, Indiana

Inquiries Invited

You, I conjure now, a full century later,
ghost hidden in these pages, along with locks
of raven hair, dried primrose, passages marked
by the pastel stains of dry-goods ribbons—

You, late visitor, showing up only at dusk,
after supper, while they sit around the stove
and by candle-light or lantern-light, begin
to read to one another—you, old necromancer,

only you, in the twilight, on a country lane,
lugging the satchel, seeing ahead the wisp
of wood smoke rising, the parlor lamp's gleam
through the willows, the barn's dark shadow.

Stay for a moment, Charlie, by the front gate,
by the phlox and the yarrow that have vanished
along with the house, the barn, the shining faces.
Tarry for a while, old wanderer, and listen.

All those books you sold from house to house
are gone now—novels and pamphlets of verse,
Emerson and Thoreau, Ruskin and Mrs. Gaskell,
all of them crumbling, dwindling into dust—

But who is calling to whom? he asks himself,
entirely conjured at last—eccentric, given
to hearing voices and paying them no mind—
yet now made real as any gingko leaf or violet

pressed for a hundred years. *O spirit,* he replies,
if in this interval we two are hand in hand,
hath not the summoner an equal need to listen?
He pauses, sets down the valise, reaches for

the gate's latch—lingers, glances around,
but discovers no reason not to go on.
There is music, not far ahead, the wheeze
of the parlor organ, the children singing

of the goose in the pond. He has arrived,
he has only to walk across the porch
and they will know his tread, the children
will rush out and take him by the hand.

And yet he is only a memory now—a card,
a half-remembered scrap of poetry
no more forceful than a book's pages
turning in the wind or a log falling to ashes.

I must leave you now, he calls, *but we shall*
gather by the river, the beautiful river.
And it is a far, far better thing that I do,
a better rest than I have ever known.

Jared Carter

What We Learn in Louisiana

It doesn't matter where you run:
the water follows, interrupts

sleep and orphaned cities.
Breaking levees, drowning
bloodlines when I was sixteen.

Teaching, always teaching:
Maybe tomorrow.

Because the young girl on the edge
contemplates on the bridge. The boat capsizes.

Priests ask to pray for peace
this season. And the rain continues
as the river threatens to bleed.

This morning, I picked up the newspaper—
the search for survivors in Port Fourchon
was ending.

The loved ones on the news flood me
for the rest of the day. Their children learn early,

water doesn't sleep; it creeps to the shore,
searching, burying the next sacrifice.

Paris Tate

On Hearing About the Tradition of Burning
the Zozobra Effigy in Santa Fe for the First Time

1. In New Orleans, I consider
the things I would give to the effigy:
a garbage bag full of pants mocking
my post-marital hips, expletives
on a piece of paper addressed to a narcissist,
a two-page estimate of repairs for the car;
a whole list of stress and gloom
I forgot about because it isn't 3 AM.

2. It's the weekend before Labor Day,
and the season slowly changes. Someone
notices the Halloween decorations in Wal-Mart
and grows impatient with the sun. Her neighbor,
and his neighbor, and his neighbor,
and their neighbor turn on the news at 6,
sigh loudly over recent family feuds, still
can't leave the dirty dishes for a better day.

3. But no one will question the woman on the Westbank
who will catch her cheating boyfriend, get a little
crazy with the gasoline and matchsticks,
set fire to T-shirts and birthday cards
until she reaches the part where relief lives.
No; No one will blame her. Secretly,
we hold letters to the unfaithful and ask to join.

Paris Tate

Lost and Found

Since lockdown, I feel I've lost my rhythm,
Out of rhyme.
I've lost some sense of priority, urgency,
Concept of time.
I don't feel I have to be so decisive. I've a tendency
to procrastinate.
I'm less punctual, less functional. More often late.
Some thoughts are less sophisticated, naïve.
I feel emancipated, more honest, I believe.
At times I'm anxious, other times still,
Yet somewhat tired.
I feel incomplete, with fractured will,
As if parts of me have become unwired.
 I rediscovered who is really important, and care what others feel, not
what they think.
Which I hope makes me more sensitive,
Stronger and less out of sync.
 By losing touch, in part, it put me in touch with my heart.
I have indeed lost touch, I have lost much, but I have also found,
That I see in a different light, lost and regained some sight,
But I still see both feet on the ground.

                              Daniel Godward

We Drift Toward Sleep

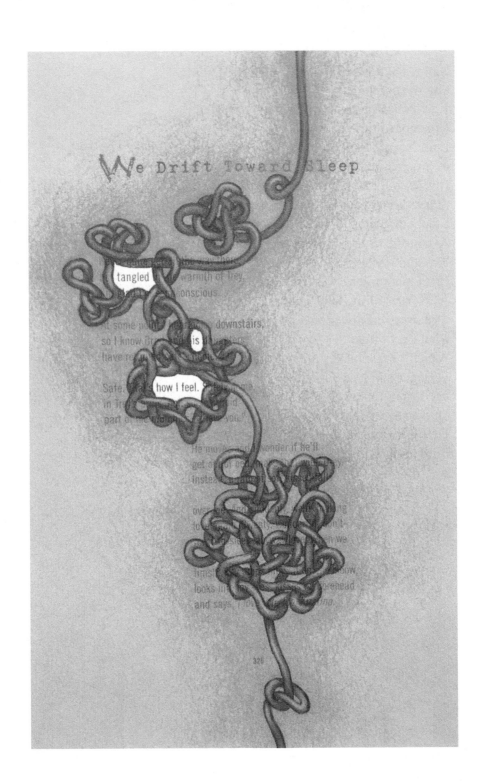

tangled

is

how I feel.

44

Between Numbers Two and Three

You came
between the numbers two and three.
I thought you might have been a girl,
but see—I did not really know.
I lost you thirty years ago.
And now, it's only when the house is full
I think of you, and you are missing,
not where you should be:
between the numbers two and three.

Now there are five,
all very much alive.
Your brothers now are uncles;
your sisters now are aunts.
The numbers jump and multiply,
and no one even has to try, and yet
I could not halt your transit.

A hole I'd feared looking through,
but you looked down and shouted *Mom.*
Come see. It's all alright. And through
that gaping place all edged with grey
that might be flesh or stone
or something that is always grey—
a glittering ballroom when I looked,
with chandeliers and girls in pink chiffon.
Not lost or gone,
but passing on
in some great endless line of love
and blood. And warmth on skin.

Lois Hambleton

Heirlooms

The monolithic curio cabinet that displays the fine china my great grandfather hauled across the ocean from Austria won't fit in my apartment. Microwave burritos don't necessitate such formality. Sterling isn't worth the cost to melt according to the pawnshop owner who also says the vintage coin collection has no appreciation beyond face value. *Don't use these in the vending machine out front*, he says, *they'll just jam up the slot*. My grandmother curated a menagerie of heirlooms that no one wants; she breathed life into stories of long-dead ancestors that no one remembers. Estate sale where everything is sold in bulk for scrap and the farmhouse is auctioned off for the twenty acres of soil with the dry creek bed at the edge. I keep what I can carry: gold plated wristwatch with a faded engraving, *To PCK on 10.29*; tarnished desk lamp; and an ornate vase.

Debris

Stop crying and jump! three floating heads taunt as they tread in the river. The boy, my father, shivers as he stands at the edge of the trestle. My grandfather jumped into that same river with his brothers, one of the only memories he had of his father laughing deep and wide. My father leaps but doesn't remember the first fall and splash. The rest of the day is sunshine and adrenaline. Sunburned, they stop at the general store for sodas. Shocked by their story, the proprietor says the wreckage of the old iron bridge rests where it collapsed in the river. Everyone laughs because no one was impaled on the rusted iron skeleton, and they were all somehow still alive.

Corpse

Heart the size of a pickup truck erupts, the whale's lungs flood like the hull of a ship. Slow descent from the surface into the deep blue darkening to black. Carcass lands on the ocean floor in a storm cloud of sediment. Ecosystems flourish around the corpse. Generations of crustaceans live their entire lightless existence inside the boundaries of the whale fall. Skeletal remains collapse, settle under the surface, disappear like they never existed. On a day like endless night, the last of the flesh is consumed, and the citizens disperse to find new homes.

Joseph Kerschbaum

How Ghosts are Born

Narrow tunnel of headlights
guides me down
this two-lane state road.
Unsure where to turn,
flash of a shadow darts
from the shoulder,
thuds under the tire.
Stopped dead in my path.
I am not the one bleeding

all over the asphalt.
On the side of the road,
darkness thick as an oil spill.
Cracked grill of the car
wheezes like an asthma attack.
Dark shape on the shore
of my high beams.
Limp paw, tail of a tan dog,
under its mouth is a spark.
Dull name tag, engraving erased,
renders the body

a John or Jane Doe.
Can't see the blood,
sticky on my fingers.
No houses in sight.
Can't go from door to door
in the middle of the night.
Best-case scenario,
this dog's owners
never travel this stretch of road.
Tell themselves & their children
animals get lost & folks take them in.
They're happy with a new family.

Or is not knowing
an injury that never heals,
a scar that stays
a mystery
cataloged in their collective narrative,
where everyone swears
when the house is quiet, dark,
they still hear scratching
at the back porch door
years later.

Joseph Kerschbaum

Black Lunch Pail

It sat on the seat of the breakfast nook
in our studio apartment on Halsted street,
dented, no longer shiny, one latch bent
with a resilience like his
that he must have learned
when he was orphaned at the age of five.
Inside, a red thermos of coffee,
one sandwich of butter and jelly
wrapped in wax paper,
an apple or orange if we had it—
every day for over 35 years,
holding the handle tight, carrying
it along like a blue-collar
man's briefcase to jobs
that were monotonous, hazardous,
dockman, slaughterhouse line-man,
giving him hernias
but gifting him with a paycheck
which he was so proud of.
It paid our bills,
bought me pretty dolls.
He never complained,
grateful for the work.
Seeing that lunch pail,
was how I knew he was home.
I would hear his comforting voice.
Oh, how I wish I had kept
that old lunch pail touched
by his calloused hands
so I could run my fingers
over it, feel his work ethic
flow into my body, keeping me going
through the rough days at my job

RM Yager

Elegy for a Thousand Books Drowned in Floodwater

This was the den.
Maneuver through stinking,
soggy sofa cushions.
Adjust your bulky mask
to deflect the poisoned air.
This was the kitchen.
Tiptoe, breath held, beside warped
interior walls. Perceive the quiet
of decomposition, black mold
on once-busy wooden spoons; wonder
at how the high water rummaged
through drawers, swiped
the heavy fruit bowl, the toaster
off the custom high counters. Run
the treacherous funhouse length
of the eat-in kitchen, take
your steps twice—toe test,
then quick and light, then next,
on buckling strips of wood;
open jaws of skewed joists below
would swallow what falls through.
This was the foyer. Move
the dank, leaden mattress that
has floated off its frame
and into the hall. Marvel at
the power of dark, quickly-
rising bayous. Smell the dead
before you see them, Homer
and H.D., Walker and Morrison,
Flannery and Eudora and Ursula,
and oh! that rare Dickinson,
Cantos and cantos and cantos,
Ezra and all his letters
to parents and poets and lovers
unbound from their soggy covers,
rotting in the northern rooms
where you slept and wrote.

Pick up the hardbound Heaney
and feel it turn to oatmeal in your hand.
Hear these books tell you what
gone forever feels like.
Remind yourself of their replaceability,
their just-thingness, but do not
believe a word of it.
Step around the mounds
of all those other authors no one
would recognize, even dry.
Watch for snakes
hiding in the pulp that was pages
and poetry flowing out of the holes
where white doors used to hang,
keeping all of you safe inside.

                              Casey Ford

I'll have to be up at the speakers table during the meal, too, but you'll know where to find me if you need me, she said, just like they were Emma's age. Lori rolled her eyes. Mom didn't seem to notice. "I'll come and get you afterward," she finished.

The other people at Chuck and Lori's table were business-people who gave them "What are you doing here?" looks and then ignored them. Lori picked at her dinner: string chicken, lumpy rice, and tough pellets of zucchini. Lori tried to imagine what a 4-H cooking judge would have to say about the meal, but that was a losing game. Lori didn't even like 4-H cooking projects anymore. Look at them because every-one did. You had to

Lori was reduced to daydreaming about whether she should take the chicken croquettes or chicken divan to the fair for non-cooking project this year when she heard an announcer say, "...our speaker for the evening..."

Lori turned around and started paying attention.

He seemed to be introducing some other person—a wildly successful businesswoman—but then he said, "Mom Lawson," and Mom stood up to a burst of applause and even a wolf whistle or two. You could tell she was standing on a stage, but the man still had to pull the microphone down for her.

"Thank you," Mom said firmly, making a motion with her hand that effectively ended the clapping. "I knew I could count on a group of bankers for a warm reception."

First Lost Things

In this order:
The house just on the other side
of the kingfisher tree tunnel.
A body that was perfectly healthy, like other kids' bodies.
The red helium balloon from the shoe store
that sold the orthopedic oxfords the doctor prescribed.

That consoling toy escaping into the roofless sky,
into the strong, healthy, playful wind,
as I tried to jump up and grab the fleeting string,
my body not fast, not sure, not buoyant enough,
while swift and lithe, the balloon flew,
becoming a red speck on a voyage
into thunderclouds over cornfields to the east,

while my mother sang, attempting to comfort,
"Up, up, and away, in my beautiful balloon,"
which made me wail louder and her laugh,
then leave me standing in the backyard of the new house,

where home was suddenly a mutable word
used for the first place I met the world
and already cannot return,
and for this *other* unchosen place,
before it means anything,
called home only because it is
where and how I have been made to live

though the wind didn't need this fading red spark,
though I wanted to hold on,
though I didn't know this loss would happen,
and there is nothing to do now
but stand here in these heavy shoes
afraid of this grief
having to let go

Liza Hyatt

Glen Helen

It comes like memories of a sea.
The feeling of home
which ribbed a child's breast.

Once, there were growing bones
and salt to learn the feelings of.

Once, in that sea,
birds were in waves,
waves in earth,
earth in bone,
and bone in water.
And from the sea
departed a flock of birds.

But what was lost is not lost.

Its pattern stretches inland with winter.
The creek rustles with brown wrinkled water,
and the bank is flocked with fallen oak leaves.
Gold nubs of old corn rows line the fields,
sun stripes the dusk with yellow waves,
and clouds are ribbed like a woman's chest.

What is being lost will not be lost.

Liza Hyatt

Lost Love Story

We found it in a Christmas tree left for weeks on the curb under dirty snow—a red bauble, metallic sheen weathering off, mirroring our faces and the world, a magic vessel that reminded us of our young but already ragged hearts. We hung it from the ceiling of our small apartment in celebration of our union, without title or dates, witnesses or blessings.

This relic went with us from cramped apartment to haunted hacienda, maid's quarters, even teepee. When you left, my heart abandoned my body. But I still had the little weathered bauble. I kept it until I learned I couldn't move on and hold on at the same time.

Then, I tried abandoning it with the garbage, but it kept returning to my doorstep.

I mailed you it and a note: *This belongs to you.* The package came back: *Return to Sender.*

I tried hammering it open. It became granite.

I tried melting it. In the hiss of flames, it froze solid.

I tried crating it up and forgetting it. Like a mouse, it gnawed through cardboard and wood.

I rubbed it like a genie's bottle. No wish-granting spirit emerged.

I put my ear to it and heard my heartbeat.

I probed it with a fishhook, snagged flesh, couldn't pull thick muscle through its slim neck.

I argued and pled, *Give me back me!* It reflected the face of a mad woman raving.

I took it to the mountains, hung it in a sighing pine, left it to wind, coyotes, shooting stars, moved five hundred miles away. Months passed. I wanted it wind-dashed to the ground in a storm, but one day a crow dropped it from gray skies into my lap.

I lived with its convenience—a heart lodged within armor chucked in the junk drawer. I went on with business, even married and dusted the old thing off, suspending it in the kitchen window to glance at while washing dishes or fighting, a symbol like a cross, but of what, I couldn't say.

I decided I'd felt the only two kinds of love. The dangerous heart-break kind, shattering glass, a fleeting cruel bubble, whose shards embed, become veteran's shrapnel, and the not-quite-right, it'll do kind, found among discards, second-hand, weather-beaten—the safe kind you wish you weren't with and wish you hadn't become. Either way, desire became an overlooked thing. Until I asked what else I might learn about love.

I took the cast-off orb down from its cobwebbed hook, held it in my hands, dusting it off, warming it, praying, waiting, waiting, left with only long, long longing, grieving for years, a stone rounded in sorrow's stream.

Until, suddenly, just now, I hear a strange pop and feel faint music growing into a deep, resonant chime. I see birth water amid silver-red sparks and glass petals floating free, disappearing. I reach up and touch wild, newborn, aching vulnerability beating in the opened window of my chest.

Now, I will live gaping, feeling everything, with no memories crowding out new moments, no symbol of what love is or was supposed to be, no guarantee that, before one of us dies, the people I love will let their own hearts be grieved free from solitary confinement.

Liza Hyatt

The Lost Discoverers

An affectionate orangutan
with an accent, I swing
with the greatest of ease
from bar to blaring bar
in the tiled Madrid night
while your *Madrileño's*
eyes dart like lizards
remembering the dark
New York subway.

Along the Paseo del Prado
we go on about the East Village
and the half-life of exile,
its public face polished
as a newly minted moon
slung into orbit
while the shadow
country slips out of reach,

a hole in the pocket
each delicious day
drops through, clanking
false as a foreign coin
in our mothers' kitchens.
Tuned into the static
between two stations,
you hate it in Spain
as I do in the States,

where years later they'll
ask, "How was your trip?"
flashing forks and knives
like the teeth of lives
unable to imagine another.
For now, we postpone the tomb
with an extended visa,

devour ourselves in fiery
mouthfuls of syntax,

and dream of a homecoming
feast, a bonfire, a wedding
orchestra when we'll fold back
the sheets on our fathers' beds
to find a boy's body grown old,
waiting for the return
of its wandering spirit.

James Nolan
for Eduardo Lago

Horizon

A hammock slung
between your extremes,
a mote of color
in the hueless you—
you who reach out
to embrace yourself

just beyond where
my eyes hope to see.
I could pursue your fierce
tendrils until I, too,
would vanish into distance
like a meridian at sea.

Tentative chimera,
fragile as the wing beat
surrounding each possible
life, its skyful
of flight surrendered
to the nowhere of you:

Should I swallow my tail
like a serpent, follow
Columbus to land's end,
or stand my ground,
American at the periscope
of all possibility?

As each wave breaks,
each head bows—
I, a child, very old—
to this . . . now,
as wild geese
through magnetic wind

are drawn in a skein
along the razor-
sharp edge
of your canceling
line between
this life

and some other.

James Nolan

Invocation with a Complaint

I have always known you,
though we haven't met.
I know how your name tastes,
though I've never said it.
You linger on the last step
of stairs I never descend.
I stand with my address book
on a landing to which you never
climb, and every day we stop
just short of each other.

I invoke you to appear,
to kiss childhood back
into my skeptical mouth,
rain into this parched air.
I invoke you at the sudden angle
of smoke, secrets, and zippers,
at the hour when earlobes,
skin along inner thighs,
a smooth chest is tenderest,
love unfolding its hammock
to fit whatever is nearest.
I invoke your breath's fur
on my neck, your curve of lips,
the sea grapes of your hair where
we'll weave a nest of lost mornings.

I'm tired of being propped up,
night's monarch, surveying
a domain as luxurious
as coffin upholstery.
I'm not cut out for such
strength of character, such
wisdom displayed under glass.

These meditative beach
walks make me mean.
This enlightened approach
is giving me a nervous rash.

I spot you in supermarket aisles.
You hover sullen and windblown
on terraces, testing the distance.
I invoke you to take aim,
to signal, present yourself
now that I've made it easier
and revealed to you my name.

James Nolan

Funeral Morning Blues

Standing in a robe at the kitchen window,
I'm pressing a shirt to wear to your funeral.
I said I'm in my bathrobe this morning,
buttoning the buttons you loved to undo.

> *Look out the window*
> *to where a continent ends.*
> *Go look out the window*
> *to where fog rolls down.*

Standing in a robe at the kitchen window,
I'm shining the shoes to carry your weight.
You hear, I'm in my damn robe this morning,
combing the hair you ran your hands through.

> *Look out the window*
> *to where youth has ended.*
> *Go look out that window*
> *to where love lies down.*

James Nolan

ors in it, the way it looked all golden somehow, stopped me. I stared at his arms and saw the Trevor that was maybe inside of the Evil Trevor, same regular boy with beautiful skin. I saw that even though he was mean and nasty, I maybe still stood up and noticed him and warned him—like I did for everybody else.

When I got to my desk, I looked up and saw the Jesus Boy looking at me. I couldn't tell what his face was trying to say—it was just blank and open and strange. I looked back at him and opened my notebook even though I didn't have to yet.

Maribel's seat was right behind mine.

"That Jesus Boy is always *looking* at you," she whispered.

"Only way you'd know is if you're always looking at him," I whispered back. I felt her poke me in the back, but ignored it.

I wrote my name at the top of the page. Beneath it, I wrote the date. Beneath that, I drew a picture of a kid on a swing. Kids said it felt like flying to jump through the air, catch onto that fence, then let yourself climb down. They said something about being up high, how it lets you see all over the place in a way that's different than looking at the world from a window. It brought me back to the day before when me and Sean were talking about those bridges he watched built. Some kids on that side of the highway were always trying to figure out ways to fly and run and cross over things and just get free or something.

Maribel was wearing a green sweater with our school's writing across the front in white letters. The sweater was too small and there were tiny lint balls on it. Everybody always caught her thinking about some other place.

Gwen

Her perfect face
a mixture of sad
& sweet lingers
in memory
along with a few
unforgettable things.

The long playlist
in her daring eyes
of all the new things
she wanted to do
before she left me
adrift in regrets.

I recall us both
staring at the mirror
where we were
too fragile in the moment,
reflecting on all
we thought beyond us.

A beautiful hiatus
when I dared time to prove
the taunting mirage of her lips
others found to be real
but I always knew
to be a false oasis.

The memories mix
aberrant playing cards
with shadowy permanence
in endless dark
of dreams begging her still
to be the light missing.

Rp Verlaine

Allure

Smirking at ambition,
we tamed desire's
sleight of hand.

Shadow dancing back
when Broadway had
undimmed bright lights.

Her mirrored shades
hid piercing turquoise eyes
vodka could not dilute.

A wicked past
replayed in dreams
she let me wander through.

A jazz score in background
playing twice as fast
till we spun out of control.

Having lived in stolen moments
we didn't know had a price
till it was long over.

Allure she had called it
before it all vanished
and now there is just …

This fall from past grace
into the arms of others
where I see just her.

Rp Verlaine

For Cassie

Living dangerously is
better than being alone
I tell the quiet hitchhiker
who I picked up far too close
to new female prison.

No new dreams of mermaids
unseen in these deep waters
crying for rescue missions
in dark turbulent waves
where I drown in regret

When I think of Cassie,
real and imagined,
everything that was said
as she poured me whiskey
in her bar with a smile.

But for a few dollars,
the toothless Puertorican lady
tells me the same fortune
I'm beginning to doubt,
of great riches and love

While the homeless vet laughs
New York rents are higher
than he was, parachuting
on brown heroin into enemy fire
in that war in Southeast Asia

Too often these nights,
I walk in the same circles
that still promise me less
than all I took for granted
and lost without honor.

It's why I treasure Cassie,
times I laughed at boredom,
pole vaulting past blurred
faces and dark lipstick lies,
taking home just her laughter
echoing still, years later.

Rp Verlaine

Late Love

As a girl
being gifted
entrusted
with wealth
to bestow upon men
I knew all feelings
giddiness
awe
naturally terror

Some days
I paused to weep
from the sheer work of it
and for the fine body
in far future
worn to bone
done with it all

Churning my mind and heart
I covered breadth
only my sex can know
and felt a woman's godliness
in my wise whimsy

And now
60 years on
I stand here bemused
ready for sleep
that's mysteriously withheld
replenishment opening my hands
new! my God
newly favored
newly knowing
in gifting
you

Dan Carpenter

Re-Lease

Oh, dear Dad, can you see me now?
I am myself like you somehow
I'll wait up in the dark for you to speak to me
How I've opened up
Release me
Release me
Release me, Dad
Release me"

— Pearl Jam, "Release"

I write my poems by hand,
slowing down the burning fever.
I think about every letter,
the memories tied to each word.
I wonder where my alter ego hides,
where the forgiveness shelters.
I imagine my father watching,
shaking his head with confusion.

I shake my head, my confusion
imagining my father watching.
I forgive my alter ego, hiding
in the wonder where I shelter.
I tie each letter to my memories,
thinking about every word.
I burn, the fever slowing down,
your hands writing my poems.

Christopher Stolle

Spring leaf grows
the tree's dream of flight.

Full forest in the stem's trunk,
branching veins set to sail.

Translucent fabric stretches warm
over summer, hovering patience.

One cool night, the dream soars,
whirling into currents of autumn sleep.

Cynthia T. Hahn
Image: Sr. Lutgardis Bonitz

Fledgling in a Japanese Garden

In a branching plum, the blue shell cracks.
Morning waves flapping against the sun.

After midday's shower, she tamps the cool,
nested moss on forested stone,
spies a wet worm emerge in tickling grass.

At dusk, stream's rolling bed awash
in misted bathing under a twisted trunk.

Within a cascade of elder cherry,
she calls evening home.

Cynthia T. Hahn

What Do We Say to the Children in the Morning?

Upstairs, the children in bed, fast asleep.
Downstairs, carnage on the television screen.
My thoughts stall because there is too much of it.
Too much mutating violence.
Too much hate tightening like a noose.
I can't help but think that from the minute
we are born, we are in for the long haul.

And what of the children upstairs,
snuggled under the bedcovers?
What do we say to them with all of this madness
gone viral, so there's no chance
they will not see it, or hear of it, or absorb it by osmosis.

Flags fly at half-mast nearly every week
denoting these small catastrophes
that have become one monstrous crisis.
Hate is hard to undo,
but not impossible.

I think of a man filmed by a news crew
at the scene of a riot,
a man just standing there,
hand to his heart.
Such a simple gesture,
full of meaning,
even as violence spored around him.

He stood there in the midst of it,
hand to his heart,
making me believe in that moment,
my trust in humankind has not been entirely annulled.

And still, it goes on, and on, and on.
The sun will come up in the morning.
Another bullet will have been fired,
another knee will have pressed down on a neck.
Upstairs, the children are tucked up in bed.
What do we say to them in the morning?

                              Kim Bolton

to do was get some wood on the fire and get *warm*. He would consider the problem of the woman later. Next month maybe, when he was sitting in his own living room with a cast on his knee and a cup of hot coffee in his hand.

He finally made it to the wood. Only four pieces were left, but they were *big* pieces. Henry might be back before they burned down, and Henry would pick up some more before going on to get he— Good old Henry, still wearing his dorky horn-rims, even in this age of soft contacts and laser surgery, but you could count on him.

Pete's mind tried to return to the Scout, crawling into the Scout and smelling the cologne Henry had not, in fact, been wearing, and he wouldn't let it. *Let's not go there*, as the kids said. As if memory was a destination. No more ghost-cologne, no more memories of Duddits. No more no bounce, no more no play. He had enough on his place already.

He threw the wood onto the fire one branch at a time, considering the pieces awkwardly, wincing at the pain in his leg but enjoying the way the sparks rose in a cloud, whirling beneath the lean-to's canted tin ceiling like crazy fireflies before winking out.

Henry would be back soon. That was the thing to hold onto. Just watch the fire blaze up and hold that thought.

No, he won't. Because things have gone wrong back at Hole in the Wall. Something to do with—

"Rick," he said, watching the flames taste the new wood. Soon they would feed and grow tall.

Clacking Past the Years

Whenever I walk into my office,
I am welcomed by the rattling rhythm
of large plastic cards
swinging on necklaces,
of small seashells wrapped
around the doorknob.
Each card comes from
a different time and place,
Most have pictures
of me wearing a younger face,
and all were passports
to new adventures.

They speak to me.
"How y'all doing?"
asks a card from
Williamsburg and
the Southern Governor's
Conference. It's just a clack away
from being pushed aside by
a media pass from Fort Wayne
that allowed me to scoot under
police crime scene tape
to view the bodies
and talk to the next-of-kin.

"Hafa dai!" shouts a card from Guam
that began two decades of beating deadlines
on foreign Far Eastern shores.
"Alii!" adds a card that gave me access
to a Paluan beach to record
Santa pushing sleds of food and toys
from the low-flying Air Force cargo plane
to the natives gathered below.

"Kumasta!" A card from the Philippines calls
in fractured Tagalog. I wore it the day
a Manila hotel lost my reservation
and gave me a free night in the Presidential Suite.
And there's that yellow pass from Okinawa
that sports a pic of a much younger me.
"Ohayo gozaimasu!" it smiles as it touches my heart.
It's where I left a family after seventeen years
gathering the news and poetry.

The cards are silent now,
and I smile sitting down
at my desk, wondering what
the newest ID card
from the Poetry Society of Indiana
will have in store.

Each card was a pass,
permission to poke
my writing stick
into piles of words
and sentences, all waiting
to be picked and pressed
onto a page to add
to my life's log.

                              David Allen

The Good Samaritan

We live in a rock bottom age,
wondering if the guy in the drug store
yelling about his right to not wear a mask may
be the next mass shooter
or if your neighbor might be
the next pandemic's patient zero.
That's what made an incident
in this small Indiana town
so unexpectedly wondrous.

On a recent weekend afternoon,
the sound of a leaf blower blasting
away two years' worth of rotting leaves,
sticks, and twigs that accumulated
while I recuperated from surgery
and as my wife battled Multiple Sclerosis
interrupted our shut-in tube binge.

My wife went outside to investigate.
"The strangest thing," she said.
"I asked him what he was doing, and
he just said he had an itch to do yardwork."
He told her that he lived down the street,
and refused any money for his labor.

Our next-door neighbor later called
and asked whether we knew the guy.
She said he shoveled her driveway
last winter without asking, which concerned her.

We didn't care, our front yard was clean.
The next day he toiled in our back yard
with his three children, again without asking.
My wife gave them bottled water as they worked
and made a special delivery of ice cream later that night.
She didn't ask if it was okay.

David Allen

maria callas in paris

the diamond collarette
is still dripping with
norma, violetta, tosca

indelible cat eyes
linger over yet
another beautiful

death on stage
a shining hour
where lucia's madness

rises out of the seine
like a crimson
revenant

or last season's
excellent rossini
it's a sunny

spring day in paris
by the bedside
there is still

a harp cadenza
inside the pearls
and the chestnut

trees still sparkle
with vocalized trills
azazel averts his

raven gaze:
let an empty theater
remain a perennial

pine-brittle accusation

Diana Thoresen

Dead Sea Stars

A rare splash of pink tentacles against the cold eternity
Hundreds of dead sea stars are gaping at

The deep blue fragments of God in Chile
The cruel bilaterian symmetry of many comets is

Burrowing in the surf zone of absolute space
Pale anemones and precious red corals

My dead star-burst biscuits, my perverse echinoderm mouths
Now the world is a loveless artistic cage

Purple and mauve carpet sea stars
Are still feeding on the red algae of a stolen heart

A blue devil fish suddenly stirred in his deep cave when
The black fire interrupted the guilloché telegraph lines

Left behind by Anne of Brittany's stormy heart in Nantes
Still embalmed, still beating, still whispering novenas

The heart is weaving red and blue silk tapestry threads
And Christ is united with Eros

The lavender Saturn is awakening again

Diana Thoresen

Burning the Boat

When we were kids, my parents got an aluminum skiff
and let my brothers and me break up our old wooden rowboat,
then burn the pieces night after night on the beach
with the help of driftwood we gathered every day.
The boat was encrusted with ancient layers of paint
and had brass fittings and screws,
so the color of the flames was always mixing and changing.
Yellow, blue, green—red was the rarest
and our favorite. We poked at the fire, transfixed,
and never realized that we had become castaways
from our childhoods. Marooned on the warm sand,
we watched Vega, Altair, and Deneb—
summer stars we thought we could steer by forever—
not noticing that they were already beginning to set.

Warren Woessner

The Dancing River

Tonight, I watch the river dancing
below the falls
in the light of the moon
reflected by ripples
that flicker and spin and change
while the veiled dancer stays
in one place and does not mind my staring.

So why should I feel sad?
From up here, I can look down
on the current almost a mile wide—
but the high banks are not stone or clay.
They are deserted downtown office buildings
and high-rise apartments
that keep watch with few lights.

I know you can never step into the same river twice,
but after the closed-for-the season sign
ice will soon put up, you can stand on it
and dance your own dance.

Warren Woessner

I paint? Who's to stop me but the brooms that have been rammed into my thin hide?"

The little dog sat listening so gravely the captain suddenly boomed a big laugh. The dog waggled his tail, swept the floor with it as he kept sitting looking up at the man. "No, you won't run away," the big man said. "Even if you've been a stray all your life, you won't run away."

He opened the door. The moonlight was so bright in the yard it seemed to fall into the house with the opening of the door. The startled little dog jumped back. The captain laughed. "I can startle you, moonlight, can't it—soft as it is."

Out in the yard, the dog, as if ashamed of his scare, raced out before the man, then came back to him in queer gyrations and circles. He made mad little nipping dashes at shadows, performed, showed off. But in the end he came back to the man to look up at his face for approval, stood looking in the footsteps.

The captain laughed and shook his head. "It's no use, I've found. It just makes you feel foolish. If you didn't learn to play when you were young, you never quite get used to it. Maybe they made us old too soon . . . . but go

Emerging Poet

The Coffee Shop home away from
greets me by name, fills my coffee
choice without difficult labels
to remember.

I sit reading Billy Collins,
Maxine Kumin, Mark Strand,
Stephen Dunn.

I want those images;
I taste their gourmet richness.

My appetite weighs me down.
I murmur how their poems flow.
Meaning and metaphor build
on their literary reputations.

At the river of my tears,
their poems already stream
into my imagination. I cry at
those words which float by me.

I can never own them.

Lee Landau

Stir Fry

He decides
the sauce is wanting,
some herb. He hurriedly adds
succulent green beans,
bitter lemon, sassy chilies
into the stir fry, so much
work to set on the table.

Nothing touches
spices already in the pan unlike
the past and future
that hold him hostage
like his marriage.

His faltering balance speaks
to daily whisky libations,
the sadness reserved for
those times when nodding off.
He sleeps and eats only
to forget a blackened house
fire, and that burnt specter
of his only child.

Lee Landau

My Father's Sword

My father's sword,
a 1910 Austrian saber,
came home with him
from World War II.

It hangs, innocent,
on my hallway wall,
glinting in the light.
A conversation piece.

I seldom think about
its bloody purpose,
human flesh it slashed,
lives it cut short.

It hangs, innocent,
my father's souvenir
from a time when
innocence was lost.

Nancy Kay Peterson

Floor Lamp

Clouds tint the evening
When they burn out

The night shift
Luminous drool of power companies

Glows over the recliner
Like an anxious parent

Suburban Coyotes

Masters of disguise,
they've been here forever.

Walking the dog
in the semi-circular light of dawn,

I expect a leer
from a threadbare coat,

the patron saints of poets
howling into the night

as though deputized
by the moon.

John Minczeski

An Incomplete History of the Mythology of Wolves

I.

A girl in red goes in search
of her grandmother.
She finds, instead, teeth.
The wolf subdued, she slits
its belly open. Grandmother
emerges, whole, unharmed.

II.

A she-wolf suckles abandoned twins.
The boys, in time, build an empire.

III.

In the English countryside,
a nobleman is bitten.
Later, in London, a man-wolf,
hungry, prowls the streets.

IV.

The gods of the earth and the gods of the sky go to war.
The Great Wolf devours the moon.
Everywhere, darkness.

William Reichard

When My Heart was a Falcon

When I was young, I was constantly hungry.
I spent my time eating, thinking of eating,
or looking for the next thing to eat.
I lacked poise. Uneasy in my body,
unsettled in my mind, I stumbled
through the long winter days
looking for what might satisfy.
My keen eyes could pick out
tiny prey, all white or brown,
from a field all white or brown.
Born with sharp sight but lacking
true vision, I starved. I swept
across the land, searching for what
I needed, but found only a lonely distance.
There was no outstretched arm,
no falconer to beckon me home.
The appearance of another bird
on the horizon was thrilling,
but I was born a solitary thing.
I wanted yet did not want.
That simultaneity cancelled out
everything, and I was left starving
again, thinking of eating or looking
for the next thing to eat.

William Reichard

"Now, Andrew!" Mr. Pu said.

Andrew stepped into Ms. Wilford's doorway. "Oh, LOOK, Ms. Wilford, LOOK!" he said in a phony-sounding voice. "There is a DEAD RAT in the HALLWAY!"

Mr. Pu groaned. "Not like *that*, Andrew!"

Ms. Wilford ran out of the room. "Andrew Flingus, if this is some sort of silly joke—"

"SURPRII I-ISE!" everyone yelled.

"Oh!" Ms. Wilford put her hand to her heart. Her mouth dropped open, "Oh, my—"

Up and down the hallway, kids and teachers burst out clapping.

"Like it?" Andrew asked.

Ms. Wilford was laughing so hard, tears streamed down her cheeks. "It's the most beautiful mural I've ever seen."

"I meant my face," Andrew said.

Ellipse

At sunrise, the heron soars effortlessly on the breeze
as waves roll in and crash into rocks and beaches,
rising tides reach high upon sands slowly fading away,
and sunlight breaks through my window and kisses my cheek.

Round and round and round the great circle of life travels,
much like a whirlpool of bubbles in a small woodland stream.
As day turns to night, and night to day while the tide rises,
as the cloudy morning brings the bell and the death bed flow.

Into autumn's burnt ashes and all the saddened masses;
it was winter's chill when my spirit lifted, my heart thrived
from a dead, frozen shard, and my soul was forever freed.
Just because you're breathing doesn't mean you're alive.

At sunset, the heron soars effortlessly into a colorful twilight,
waves whisper to the rocks and sandy beaches,
great tides fall slowly as the full moon rises in a pink sky,
a lullaby rocks me to sleep as moonlight kisses my cheek.

Ken Allan Dronsfield

Equilibrium

Why do we sail?
Why set off towards a horizon
that shall never be reached?
Adrift in this unforgiving sea,
a universe of blinding fog, horizontal
rains and picture-perfect days;
to stop would be to die a slow death.
We sail close-hauled, cruising
in only thirty degrees of wind.
It's a perfect equilibrium,
a true symphony of the mind and soul,
of our wants versus our needs,
between the forces of wind in the sails,
the weight of the keel, and held only by
the laws of gravity.
Yes, an orchestration in the center
of the infinite blue waters.
The horizon is always my destiny,
sailing my deepest love.
A never-ending journey waits for no man,
only the winds.

Ken Allan Dronsfield

Raker Gauge

Found inside the wall of an old farmhouse
bought from those who homesteaded here
for generations, the strange device was a mystery.
Stamped nineteen eleven and lost a century,
it was, the craft sawyer said, a raker gauge, used to set
the height of the rakers on a crosscut saw—
the saw itself an elegant design, its cutting teeth
spaced with rakers that scoop the sawdust
from the cut as the saw passes through,
a precise and fluid motion when teeth and rakers
are filed at proper height and angle, the gauge
as guide to sharpening, lying smoothly along
the saw ridge like a woman leaning
against the kitchen counter, reaching high
to the cupboard for a dish, the line of her body
straight and true, the simple task a work of beauty.
Antique ways slip by as invention builds
upon itself with sure momentum. Laser cutter
supplants crosscut saw and raker gauge,
and the labor of hands becomes a memory.

Thomas Alan Orr

Of all the things I've lost,
two haunt me still. Two
poems that perhaps weren't
ever written, but that I've lost
just the same. I do remember
pacing the floor for both,
composing all night,
chain-smoking, sweating.
One, the first serious poem

I ever took a shot at;
second, a poem I wrote
without hearing words,
catching the images pure …
on … was it on lined paper,
as I remember? Something I
never use if I have a choice.
Or was it in a notebook that

somehow I've forgotten?
Both poems felt real to me—
though the first was only
a mix of The Doors
and *The Waste Land*.
It felt so real to be writing
on a hot summer night of
"a Roman wilderness of pain"

and "these fragments I have
shored against my ruins."

And the other night,
stick figures and gasoline
and the shadowed outlines
of two people who would be
lost to me, as lost as those
poems that perhaps never were.

Images lost in the darkness.

Rev. Dr. David Breeden

What We Lost at the Airport

I got to the airport early
after a long week
of soaking in people,
liturgies, and litanies of stories
in the name of our Creator.

I got to the airport early
to be alone
in the row of chairs facing the wall
but next to the window,
and hoped you couldn't see me.
I'd been seen enough for one week.

I got to the airport early,
remembering that when I was a little girl
we'd go to the airport early
and wait at the gate for my dad.
We'd sit in these same chairs,
look out these same windows,
watch his plane land,
and wait for him to exit the jetway
with a hug and a token to remember that he'd come home to us.

Once, he brought me a statue of the Washington Monument,
golden,
and it sat on my desk
throughout school and college
and my first apartment in Poughkeepsie,
but I lost it somehow, somewhere along my way,
and little girls can't wait at the gate anymore
for their dad to come home,
can they?

I went to the airport early
to be alone.
Outside the window
where I expected to see planes
was a butterfly,
golden,
trying to catch my attention.
Not because she was vain
or a kind of token,
but because she's beautiful
and she waits
for little girls' fathers to arrive.

She wanted me to know.

Teri Harroun

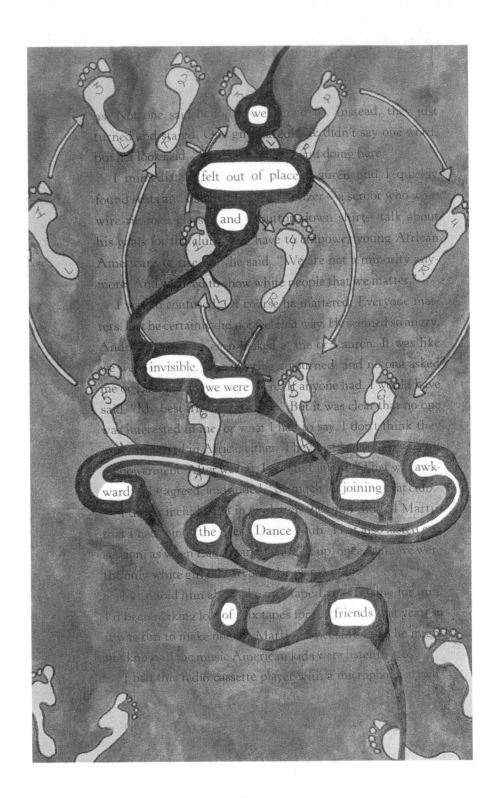

we felt out of place and invisible. we were awkward joining the Dance the of friends

Pressed

That moment
when confusion falls away—
the realization,
the scent of yesterday's flower,
decay,
the clarity
that everything will leave us
behind.
We are the flower,
our blooming moment
come and gone.
Our only grace
that someone will press us
between the pages of a beloved book,
and we'll be remembered then,
discovered in the rustling,
a moment of happenstance.

John Hinton

To Serenity

I am here, but gone,
present, but no longer remaining;
hiding in plain sight.
I am everywhere and nowhere,
in hours redeemed and hours lost.
I am the yellow, faded photograph—
the color of once upon a time.
I am a conspirator with elements,
rust that tarnishes
on a teasingly warm late autumn day.
I am the unexpected postcard of cold regards,
the sepia seduction
luring today into yesterday's bed.
Do you see me?
I am the haze that distorts,
making memories something more,
something less.
I am the passing, taking, erasing.
Existing in shadow, lurking in light.
I am the either/or, the neither/nor,
the firefly's glow, the mosquito's bite.
Have you forgotten to remember me?
Do you see me yet?
I am here,
gone,
present, but no longer remaining.
I am hiding in plain sight.

Did you see me
when I had momentarily
stepped from the shadows?
You involuntarily blinked,
and I am seen no more again.
But tell me …
did you recognize me?

John Hinton

Frank and Dorothy

died within two months of one another,
his departure first, his body
a durable wooden boat, steadfast and indefatigable, and she,
his steadfast mooring for more than sixty years.
He sank slowly, his heart taking on water,
its chamber unable to bilge that lethal tide.
Separated from him first by miles and then by death,
she lingered a while,
her own body a great weight that neither she nor anyone else
could lift above the rising water line.
She met that solitude belligerently.

Her life before him was not a life
of joy or even the meanest economy. I know very little
of how she spent her childhood hours or counted
those adolescent minutes ticking slowly as for most girls
and holding, always, the potential for anguish.
The fact that she spoke so little of her family and only
through tight lips told me everything she wanted me to know.
So when he died, she simply went limp,
asking my father why Frank hadn't come to see her
in so many days. All time reduced
to the span of his absence. Naively, we imagined
she had forgotten he died, the brown waters of dementia
obscuring this truth. But the truth was
she simply couldn't tolerate a day without him in it.

What does a woman like this do?
She shakes her fist and refuses to stay a moment longer.
I think of them, their life together as ordinary
as a jam sandwich, and I hunger for their daily meal—
a round table unadorned, sugared coffee
and toast with someone who knows whether I'll want
one slice, one spoon, or two.

Deborah Zarka Miller

Under the Porch Light

If we let our minds drift
to the beginning of our love,
perhaps we can see how
it shaped us, how we were
sculpted by bliss and the
fear of it, the opening up
of ourselves to it, how we both
lay down, at times, and let it
wash over us.

You kissed me
under a porch light many
years ago, a quick,
solemn movement, yet it
bound me to you. I can
show you the layers of such
moments, how they
kept me near you all
these years. It was never
the spectacular or the perfect,
rather the simplest of motions,
like your lips to mine.

                    Mary Sexson

The Grammar of Love

I caught the second wind of my life
sometime in my forties,
when our love became more
than a common noun, and we found
a path back to each other's
way of thinking.
There were days of weeping,
certainly, mixed
with the remnants of our spite,
threatening us both
with the notion of losing
all over again.

But we rose each day
through the murky waters of resolution,
restless for the touch of each other
and the sounds
of our soothing voices,

a resurrection of what was lost
laid before us.

And our love became the predicate,
stated in the nominative case:

Love is bitterness.
Love is redemptive.
Love is grace.

Mary Sexson

Untangling Lines

The dangling poem
contemplates her lips,
instinctively aligning,
as if Moby Dick
spotted the *Pequod,*
weighing the juicy hyperbole
measured
by picked bones left behind.
Should she probe the words
she softly plucks
like ukuleles wailing
twing-twang conversations
waxing her sentimental,
or should she playfully enjamb
her lines with a twist
of pineapple
crushed
against the pina colada skies,
satisfying her taste
for sweet simile
smothered in mixed metaphor?

Lylanne Musselman

True Love

"I Will Always Love You" brings me to tears,
sung either by the original Dolly Parton
or the heartbreaking Whitney Houston.

It takes me back to when I was in love,
a love so good, I never suspected it was bad.
The love of my life was unavailable to me every day
since he lived near the Chesapeake Bay and
I in landlocked Indiana.

We made it work with our own kind of magic
for five wonderous years, until I found out he wasn't
officially divorced. Still, the bittersweet memories
come around without warning, and they're
all I carry with me.

Could we have made it until death do us part?
I found out he died four years ago. My heart sunk.
Now I'll never know anything truer than us
no matter how hard I've tried to forget him.
He was my one.

Lylanne Musselman

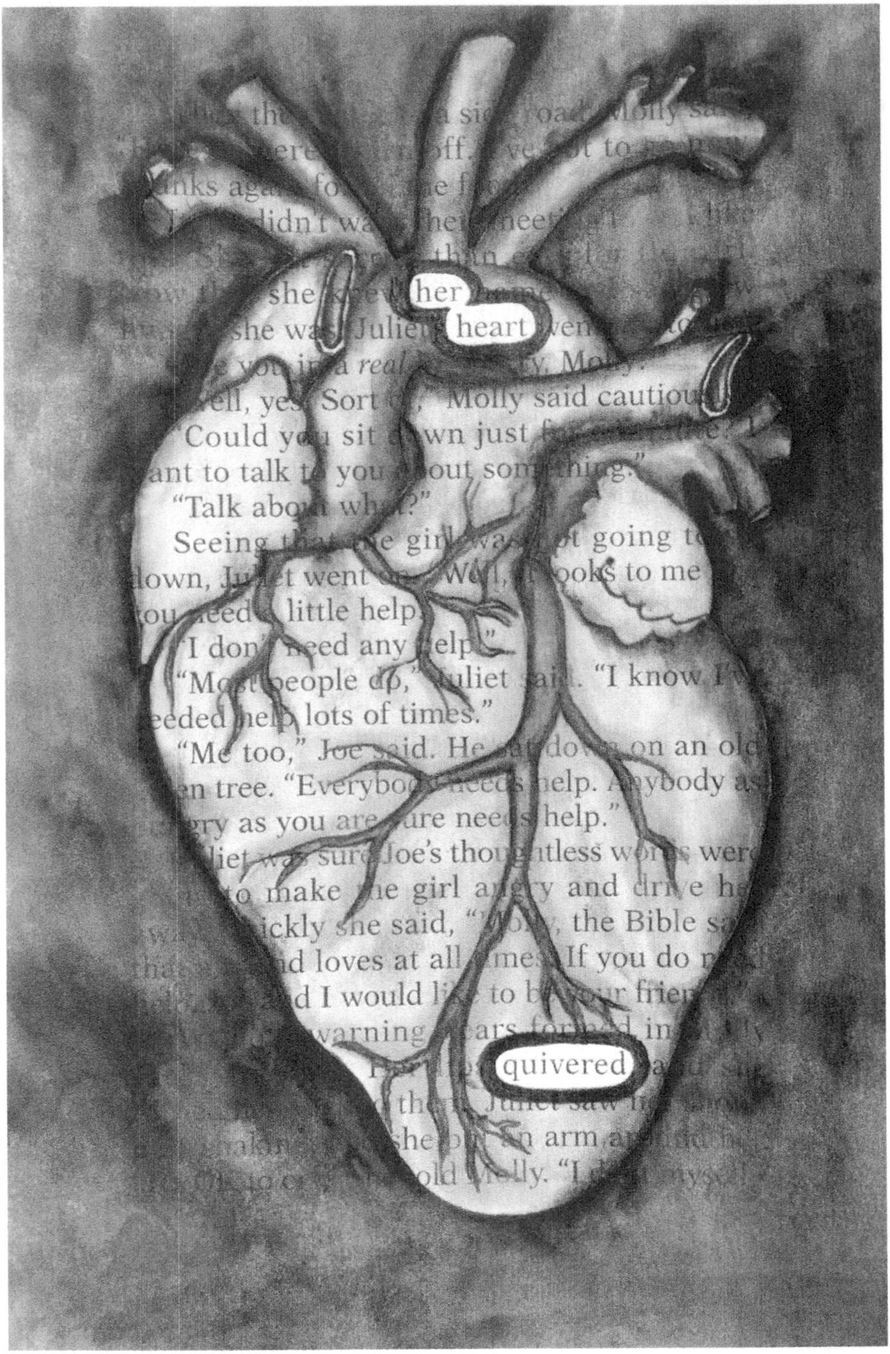
her
heart
quivered

Preserved

Trying write on the subject of time,
I realize nearly all my poems are about time
in one way or another—
trying to capture the ephemeral moment,
the grains of our existence that together make a life,
trying to encase in amber or in iron
something as brief and fleeting
as the heartbeat of a hummingbird.

I often question if time even exists,
or if the universe began when I was born
and ceases when I die—
which, of course, it does.
But I read old books,
meet old portraits eye to eye,
listen to the last castrato sing a terrible lament
on a century-old recording,
so I know there are other lives,
other universes that overlap my own.
Maimonides said that in preserving a single life,
all life is preserved.
Perhaps if I can preserve a moment,
every moment might last forever somewhere
in a place called Time

Patrick Kalahar

Notes Toward the Writing of a Poem

First you must have meaning,
the elusive and hidden beast
hovering at the periphery
of an almost remembered dream.

Then you must have shape and form,
words fashioned in the way of Hephaestus
from metal and fire,
with images that can stop the breath.

And you must have rhythm
even if without rhyme or meter.
A poem must pulse
like a drum or blood in a vein,
and be felt and tasted on your tongue.

A poem can change the world,
or change ourselves,
alter our perceptions with new constructs,
creating synapses,
impulses of cunning revelation
that lead us to other realities.

This is not a poem,
but only notes toward a poem
I hope I might write someday.

Patrick Kalahar

Driving Oklahoma

Driving Highway 44 to Tulsa,
I pass Lone Elk Park and realize
if I had started the trip hours earlier
yesterday, I would not be here now,

but somewhere else if I held steady,
didn't waver or deviate from the route
which I track now through seemingly
endless means to unintended destinations.

Looking back at myself tomorrow,
I could be ahead of schedule, driving
past those enormous green signs that read,
DO NOT DRIVE INTO SMOKE—

a magical directive that curves into the pit
of my stomach as I cross Big Piney Creek,
latticed in the October bones of sycamore,
dogtooth violets napping in the red clay.

Near the horizon, finally catching up
with myself, smoke meets the roadway
in a mysterious vanishing act of driving.
Stories trail off under a burnished sky.

Men are buried here for hazy reasons.
Cows turn heavy heads now, slowly
in my direction, appearing guilty
as much as cows are able.

Stephen R. Roberts

Publication Countdown

I write a four-page love letter to a woman I believe
believes in my love and in turn loves me despite my faults,
misdemeanors, shortcomings, and absent-minded shenanigans.

I prepare a batch of poems for a renowned publication
only poets know, a rich sampling of my work including
humor, pathos, nature's eccentricities, questions without answers.

I pack them into envelopes in a state of perpetual anxiety.
Print clearly, short-change the postal service, reverse addresses,
pop them in the red and blue box on a misnamed street, and wait.

Three weeks later, I receive an acceptance, my love letter taken
for publication. The highly regarded review commenting,
"We loved this silly madness
and your propensity to reveal your ignorance of the world."

I never again hear from the loved woman who loved me.
Not so much as a note. So what is love if not misunderstanding?
What is loss if not five unreturned poems, four published love thoughts,
three threats from the post office, no more two of us, only one? Me.
But I'm published, by God.
Or at least by a respectable literary periodical.

Stephen R. Roberts

Grandad's Phone

An antique phone adorns the wall
next to the desk in my study,
the wood in places now dry and warped,
not like when new at Grandad's house.
It was the era of party lines;
our ring back then one long, one short.

We knew at times old Minnie listened in,
the nosy neighborhood publicist.
Grandad was always sparse with words,
so little for gossip of any worth.

Some days I lift that worn receiver
and press it tightly to my ear.
Oh, dear Grandad, have you hung up,
or are you simply being terse?

Joe Ottinger

Evelyn's Barrette

On a trip to visit my son,
I lose a keepsake.
I must have taken it
out of my hair in the car,
laid it in my lap,
dropped it at night
when I got out.

The next morning,
I retrace my steps,
but trash cans
pulled out into the street
make it impossible to
search where I had parked.

It was the item I picked
when a poetry prompt asked,
"What is the one thing you would
run back into a burning house to get?"
It was a birthday gift from a friend
long gone, a piece of my past
I hang on to like that thread
of Stafford's. A few months later,

an email from my son asks
"Is this yours? I found it
under the coffee table when I vacuumed."
I remember unclasping it to lie back,
to do some stretches on the floor.

Next time I visit,
I retrieve the barrette,
making no comment
about my son's
housekeeping.

Jan Chronister

The Moon is a Dream Catcher

Inspired by Anna Z Ill's *Soft Moon Rising*

I have strange, terrible dreams,
but they recede,
they disappear, and I can't catch them.

If you can't catch them,
how do you know they're strange and terrible?

Because I wake up sad.

I dream about an imaginary city.
Sometimes I walk through it,
sometimes I drive
or even fly over it.
But I know its neighborhoods.
It's unsettling, but familiar.

Do your feet hurt when you wake up?
Are you out of gas?
Are you blinded by the moonlight?

No. I like dreaming ... having dreamt.
Even when I can't remember details,
I like having been somewhere ... else.

And I like waking up to your soft green face smiling at me.

Our dreams rise through us like the moon,
and you keep me green and new.

Like your beautiful face.
We're three-quarters of the way to our final dream.

I love your sweet lunacy.
Our night flights carry us above the ordinary.

Good that the strange and the awful vanish.
I'll fly along with you in your green dreams.

We'll catch them together.

And bring them back.

Deborah Ann Percy & Arnold Johnston

Winter Afternoons

Remember the winter afternoon
we went to the spot I'd discovered
with the view of the sycamores
on the slope
rising above Fall Creek?

Too cold for me to struggle
with pushing your chair up the path,
we settled into
a picnic in the car,
watching sun throw shadows
on the white bark of the trees.

Unable to hold your body upright
more than a short while,
you were leaning into the armrest between us
eating your cashews.

When you looked at me
with that radiant smile
that told me you were savoring the moment,
time paused for us
and we had all we needed.

Today I walked the trail there,
breathing in bare trees
and cold air …

Was that you,
gliding easily beside me,
beckoning me to quicken my pace,
to join you in your joy?

Rosanne Megenity Peters

Giving His Body to the Lake He Loved

After six months of the comfort
of having his remains on the mantel,
I pick up the urn,
a screwdriver to open it,
a book of Mary Oliver poems,
and drive to the lake.

The walk to the dock is brisk.
Hugging the precious vessel close,
I step onto the swaying wood platform,
climb into a rented boat,
and set out across the choppy water.

I want to be in the center,
away from all shorelines;
nothing close or confining for this body,
reduced in his final years
from robust professor
to helpless frailty.

After singing, asking country roads
to take him home,
I open the urn and
study fine alabaster ashes.

Scooping up a handful,
I hold them near the wavy water
and slowly open my fingers.

Like a trail of pale gray smoke,
they blow backward
before touching water with a whispered hiss,
an instant of effervescence before sinking.

Again and again I do this,
feeling his spirit's joy
as his body is freed.

When it's complete,
I sit quietly,
allowing my boat to drift.

Silently, an eagle rises from the treetops,
twice circles the area
where the relics are dispersing,
then ascends high above the horizon
and departs.

Silence is broken by a fish leaping from the water
to shimmer for a moment,
then descends and disappears.

The woman I was—
wife, lover, nurse/companion—
likewise vanishing.

The passage he and I shared,
roving this beautiful
unbearable world together,
gone as well.

All dissolving like him,
back to the body
of the numinous.

                                        Rosanne Megenity Peters

Ephemera

I fell asleep
writing out the words
I dreamed
I could share.

They were perfect.
Stunningly succinct
in their Sunday best.

I was so excited
I woke,
a willing scribe.
My mission
so bold.
But my dreams were just vapors.
The only mark on the paper
was the scribble I'd scratched
in the midst of my nap.

But, if you could have seen …

Chris Hasara

Haikus

Poem in my hand
My signature on a page
I don't recall writing

Holding a photo
A day of joyful faces
You can't remember

Playing in my mind
I notice forgotten tunes
Playing in my mind

Chuck Kellum

Morning splinters into shoal reefs.

We waken to graves,
A tide of weather and early hair,

A window of volcanoes,
Purple blue mist,
A seal cackling near driftwood.

Michael H. Brownstein

Loss & the Becoming

Among extensive oaks and ash,
with bare bones for limbs extended toward heaven to beg
or praise unseen entities, I weep
for the loss of my caregiver.
Where is the guiding branch
to lead me through this maze
filled with a mist
that hides escaping paths?
A figure stands erect;
a silhouette of the deceased.
Hopeful feet carry me
in directions not on the map
my mother gave before
she passed away.
Neither I nor she know
what's to become
of this forest
we've called home
when the mist turns
to smoke and all we
feel are flames.

Tim Heerdink

If Karma Came in Stages

Are you as surprised as I am
that Karma can come in stages
and span 40 years,
then bite you
in the amends long ignored?

Pissed off, I directed the venom
to the gathering cloud of blame:
Fault! Payback!
Not me, the victim, surely.

I vacillated
between revenge and promise,
sweet return on what I invested
as a wounded warrior.

Years passed.
I licked my wounds,
damaged soul
alone in the cesspool

and you finally came, Karma,
not to avenge the wrongs,
but to heal the survivor
through suffering of the favored one.

Recognizing pain now received
was pain I once delivered,
this crone is now a guide, and
Karma, not avenger but
teacher and healer

KJ Carter

you undid me. my eyes star- ing at my unraveling

...seemed... and all the time...

Anyway, when I would... all... two years, then I'd...
...I'd... back a... different...
...greenhouse... That's when I'd...
...up early... would have changed... a year...
...for us...

you... correct... undid the year you met

...it would undo the year... having... right?" I

glanced at her out of the corner of my eyes.

Mom looks... smaller than usual, like she would break if you touched her. Her face is thoughtful and she leans... back in her... But her hands... playing ...les and perhaps her... maybe... a little kid star- ing... at the porch... ...braced to catch... in case she falls over.

"Nope, never," she says... and... words aren't big and dramatic, but come... bright... thinking. "I never walked the blocks without you in my plan. Never, Danny. You... my family."

Her walking game sort of re... about... I... so I tell her about Penelope weaving a... unraveling tapestry, but Mom just gets that happy look on her face ...she thinks of me getting my good Bradshaw edu- cation.

David Allen grew up on Long Island and traveled the world after spending a tour in the Navy. He is a retired journalist, spending nearly four decades

on newspapers in New York, Virginia, Indiana, and the Far East. He a member of the Last Stanza Poetry Association and the Poetry Society of Indiana, where he served as vice president and contest director. He has been published in many online and print journals, and has three books of poetry available from Amazon: *The Story So Far, (more),* and *Type Dancing.* Visit his blog at www.davidallenpoet.net.

Lois Baer Barr lives in Riverwoods, Illinois with her husband Lew and their pandemic puppy. She has had wonderful women role models in her

life, especially her mother, Ethel Cooper Baer, and mother-in-law, Lillian G. Barr. They were both short, both teachers, both grew up speaking Yiddish with their parents, both married lawyers. Their differences stemmed from Mom's Louisville accent and manners and Lillian's Newark, New Jersey ways. But they became fast friends over many a Scotch on the rocks. Two stories about my mother were published by *The Jewish Literary Review*, an online journal, and another, "War Stories," appeared online at *Flashquake* before she died. She was thrilled when it received a Pushcart nomination.

Heather A. Smith Blaha is an 8th grade teacher and artist. She has illustrated the book *The Fig Tree* by Ron Ringenburg. Most of her art is

inspired by things most others consider trash to be tossed away. She utilizes trash to inspire as well as provide the materials for her works. She sees beauty and potential beyond the items' original purposes. She strives to help others see beauty and value where and when it exists in ways that culture often rejects or overlooks. Her blackout poetry joins voice and images to tell stories more powerfully than either words or pictures alone could do. She searches a damaged book for words she feels fit together for a poem, then inks them and draws or paints the background. For her, creating art is an act of transformation or redemption, giving new life to objects and materials and helping people see these things in new ways. For more of her work in full color, find her on Instagram @LastNightIMade

Kimberly Anne Bolton is the author of two books of narrative poetry, *Folk* (2018) and *Tales from Grindstone Creek* (2020). Her narrative poem "The  Tale of Mercy Periwinkle" was presented as a theatrical production in November 2019. In the spring of 2019, her poem, "Tattoo" was published in the annual Poetry Super Highway online issue of *Yom Hashoah*. She is a graduate of Columbia College. She lives in Jefferson City, Missouri near her beloved Missouri River with her significant other, David Marthers. Kimberly is currently working on her third book of poetry *Trees and Broomsticks*.

Sr. Lutgardis Bonitz OSB, a Benedictine nun at St. Hildegard Abbey in Germany, finds spiritual resonance in nature. Her photography captures the divine spark in form, textures and/or colors she finds in the garden and grounds she tends.

James H Bowden, PhD, is retired from the Indiana University system where he was a Professor of English. His publications include a Twayne series book, *Peter DeVries, a*  *Critical Study*, and a novel and a book of short stories (*Rêve Américain* and *Don't Lose This, It's My only Copy*) under the pen name Greenfield Jones. He has three sons, one stepdaughter, and ten grandchildren, and is long retired from IU Southeast, which sent him to teach in China, Malaysia, Saudi Arabia, and Poland. He also spent time in Korea, France, and Uruguay.

Jonathan Bracker's poems have appeared in *The New Yorker, Poetry Northwest, Southern Poetry Review*, and other periodicals, and in eight collections, the latest of which, from Seven Kitchens Press, is *Attending Junior High.*

David Breeden has written and published several books of poetry and 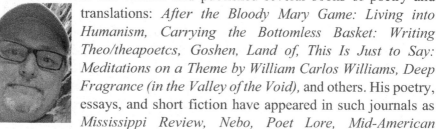 translations: *After the Bloody Mary Game: Living into Humanism, Carrying the Bottomless Basket: Writing Theo/theapoetcs, Goshen, Land of, This Is Just to Say: Meditations on a Theme by William Carlos Williams, Deep Fragrance (in the Valley of the Void)*, and others. His poetry, essays, and short fiction have appeared in such journals as *Mississippi Review, Nebo, Poet Lore, Mid-American Review, North Atlantic Review, Boston Literary Review, Turnstile, Nidus,* and *Paragraph.* He lives in Minneapolis.   davidbreeden7.medium.com

Michael Brockley is a retired school psychologist who lives in Muncie,

Indiana. His poems have appeared in *Fatal Flaw, Last Stanza Poetry Journal,* and *Visiting Bob: Poems Inspired by the Life and Work of Bob Dylan.* Poems are forthcoming in *Woolgathering Review, Flying Island,* and the *Indianapolis Anthology.*

Debbi Brody is an avid attendee and leader of poetry workshops

throughout the Southwest. She has been published in numerous international, national and regional journals, magazines and anthologies of note. Her newest full length poetry book, *In Everything, Birds,* (Village Books Press) and her recent chapbook, *Walking the Arroyo,* are available at independent bookstores across the US, the usual online sources, from the author at artqueen58@aol.com, and through the publisher.

Michael H. Brownstein has been widely published throughout the small and literary presses. His work has appeared in *The Café Review, American Letters and Commentary, Skidrow Penthouse, Xavier Review, Hotel Amerika, Free Lunch, Meridian Anthology of Contemporary Poetry, The Pacific Review, Poetrysuperhighway.com* and others. In addition, he has

nine poetry chapbooks including *The Shooting Gallery* (Samidat Press, 1987), *Poems from the Body Bag* (Ommation Press, 1988), *A Period of Trees* (Snark Press, 2004), *What Stone Is* (Fractal Edge Press, 2005), *I Was a Teacher Once* (Ten Page Press, 2011) and *Firestorm: A Rendering of Torah* (Camel Saloon Press,

2012). His latest volumes of poetry, *A Slipknot to Somewhere Else* (2018) and *How Do We Create Love?* (2019), were recently released (Cholla Needles Press).

Dan Carpenter is a poet, fiction writer, freelance journalist, and former

Indianapolis Star columnist. He has published poems and stories in many journals and is the author of two collections of poems, *More Than I Could See* (Restoration Press) and *The Art He'd Sell for Love* (Cherry Grove Collections).

Jared Carter's seventh collection of poems, *The Land Itself*, is from Monongahela Books in West Virginia. He lives in Indianapolis.

K J Carter (Kathy Jo) got an early start in the printed word. Retired urse educator, musician, animal lover and poet. Blessed to be a part of the Last Stanza Poetry Association family and a member of the Poetry Society of Indiana and the National Federation of State Poetry Societies. The cherry on her sundae is being a great-grandmother.

Jan Chronister lives in northern Wisconsin within sight of Lake Superior.

She currently serves as president of Wisconsin Fellowship of Poets. Jan has published two full-length poetry collections and four chapbooks.
http://www.janchronisterpoetry.wordpress.com

Ken Allan Dronsfield is a disabled military veteran and poet from New Hampshire, now residing in Oklahoma. He has six poetry collections to date: *The Cellaring, A Taint of Pity, Zephyr's Whisper, The Cellaring, Second Edition, Sonnets and Scribbles,* and *Inamorata at Twilight*. Ken loves hiking, thunderstorms, and spending time with his rescue cats Willa and Yumpy.

Bruce Ducker's numerous poems and stories have been published in leading journals, including in *The New Republic; the Yale, Southern, Sewanee, Literary, American Literary, Missouri,* and *Hudson Reviews; Shenandoah; Commonweal; the New York Quarterly; the PEN/America Journal;* and *Poetry Magazine*. The prize-winning author of eight novels and a book of short fictions, he lives in Colorado.

In 2022, **Casey Ford** will complete a Fairfield University MFA in creative writing with an emphasis in poetry. She is an instructor of English at Lamar University in Beaumont, Texas, with research interests in word and music studies. Her poetry has appeared in *Concho River Review, Amarillo Bay,* and *Writing Texas,* among others.

Daniel Godward was born in Limehouse, East London, to a poor working-

class family. He enjoys reading and began writing poetry from an early age, inspired by the nonsense verse of Edward Lear and Lewis Carroll. He then turned a part-time acting job into a career, following his passion. He has had small roles in feature films and lead roles in small films. He has always written poetry in his spare time and now has a Facebook page (Danny Godward Poetry) devoted to his writing. Daniel is the author of *The Ant and the Elephant* and *The Journey*. He and his loving wife live in Kent, SE England, and they have three grown children all living abroad.

James Green has worked as a naval officer, deputy sheriff, high school English teacher, professor of education, and administrator in both public schools and universities. His academic publications include three books, as well as scores of articles in professional journals. He has published four poetry chapbooks, and individual poems have appeared in literary journals in the USA, UK, and Ireland. Recipient of numerous awards for his poetry, his

most recent collection, *Long Journey Home*, was named winner of the 2019 Charles Dickson Chapbook Contest sponsored by the Georgia Poetry Society. He is a member of Last Stanza Poetry Association.

Cynthia T. Hahn, Professor of French at Lake Forest College, where she teaches creative writing and translation, is the author of two books of poetry, *Outside-In-Sideout* (Finishing Line Press, 2011) and a self-translated bilingual (French-English) volume, *Co-ïncidences,* illustrated by Monique Loubet (alfAbarre Press, 2014). She also plays bass ukulele and West African drums and loves to play with sound and rhythms.

Lois Hambleton is from Solihull in the West Midlands, UK. She studied Literary & Cultural Studies at the University of Warwick and Education at Birmingham City University. She has work included in - *Last Stanza Poetry Journal* (2020), *A Wild and Precious Life,* a recovery anthology *(*Unbound 2021*), PB9 The Covid Diaries (Poetry Bus Magazine 2021)* and *Dear Dylan, Letters to, and poems after, Dylan Thomas (*Indigo Dreams Publishing 2021).

Fr. Teri Harroun is a gluten-free gummy-bear loving poet, parent, and priest. She serves as pastor and Poet Laureate at Light of Christ in Longmont, Colorado,  and enjoys reading, crocheting, walking, and moose-ology (all the things you learn about God when you get yourself caught between a mama moose and her babies). Her book of poetry is available on Amazon: *A Woman Called Father: Reflections of Priesthood in a Woman's Body.*

Chris Hasara is a part-time poet and father of four from Northwest Indiana. He has been fascinated by tales of the weird (Poe, Bradbury, King) from an early age. Time spent farming and gardening has made him suspicious of plants.

Tim Heerdink is the author of *Somniloquy & Trauma in the Knottseau Well, The Human Remains, Red Flag and Other Poems, Razed Monuments, Checking Tickets* *on Oumaumua, Sailing the Edge of Time, I Hear a Siren's Call, Ghost Map, A Cacophony of Birds in the House of Dread,* and short stories, *The Tithing of Man* and *HEA-VEN2.* His poems appear in various journals and anthologies. He is the President of Midwest Writers Guild of Evansville, Indiana.

John R. Hinton is an Indiana poet and writer. His writing is inspired by our daily human interactions and the accompanying emotions: love, hate,  indifference, passion. His words explore who we are, how we behave. Sometimes eloquent, other times gritty, these words seek to reveal the joy and pain of living this beautiful human existence. He is the author of two poetry collections: *Blackbird Songs* and *Held.* John is the Vice President of the Poetry Society of Indiana and a member of Last Stanza Poetry Association.

Peter Huggins is the author of seven books of poems, including the forthcoming *Small Mercies. Audubon's Engraver* and *South* were shortlisted for the International Rubery Book Award. He has also published three books of fiction for children. *Trosclair and the Alligator* appeared on the PBS show *Between the Lions.* A recipient of a Literature Fellowship in Poetry from the Alabama State Council on the Arts, he taught for thirty-one years in the English Department at Auburn University.

Joseph Hutchison, Colorado Poet Laureate (2014-2019), has published 17 poetry collections, including *The World As Is: New & Selected Poems, 1972-2015*; *Marked Men;* and *Bed of Coals* (Colorado Poetry Award winner). His poetry, fiction, and essays have  appeared in many anthologies and over 100 journals, including *Agni Review, Cutthroat, Kentucky Review, Pedestal Magazine, Poetry* (Chicago), and *Poetry Salzburg Review*. His latest collection, *Under Sleep's New Moon*, is forthcoming in Summer 2021 from NYQ Books. Photo by Kim Anderson.

Liza Hyatt is a poet whose books include *Once, There Was a Canal* (Chatter House Press, 2017), *The Mother Poems* (Chatter House Press, 2014), *Under My Skin,* (WordTech Editions, 2012), *Seasons of the Star Planted Garden* (Stonework Press,  1999), and *Stories Made of World* (Finishing Line Press, 2013). She received an Individual Arts Project Grant from the Indiana Arts Commission to research Irish immigrant family history in 19th century Indiana. This research led to the poems in *Once, There Was a Canal*. She is a 2017 recipient of the Creative Renewal Arts Fellowship from the Indianapolis Arts Council. Liza is an art therapist at IU Health Charis Center for Eating Disorders. She is an adjunct professor in the Art Therapy Master's program at St. Mary of the Woods College. She also provides dreamwork and spiritual guidance using expressive arts and inter-spiritual practices. Her blog Soulfaring: Imagination's Homing Journey through Art, Poetry and Dreams can be found at www.lizahyatt.com

Michael Lee Johnson lived ten years in Canada during the Vietnam era and is a dual citizen of the United States and Canada. He is a poet, freelance  writer, amateur photographer, and small business owner in Itasca, Illinois. Mr. Johnson is published in more than 2033 new publications in forty-one countries. He edits and publishes ten poetry sites. He is the administrator of six Facebook poetry groups and has several new poetry chapbooks coming out soon. He has over 533 published poems to date, and has been nominated for two Pushcart Prize awards, poetry 2015/1 Best of the Net, 2016/2 Best of the Net 2017, 2 Best of the Net 2018.

Married writers **Deborah Ann Percy (Johnston)** and **Arnold Johnston** live in Kalamazoo and South Haven, MI. Their plays (written separately and jointly) have won over 300 productions and readings on stage, screen, and radio, as well as numerous awards and publications across the country and internationally; and they've written, co-written, edited, or translated some twenty books. Their  award-winning poetry, fiction, non-fiction, and translations have appeared widely in literary journals and anthologies. After a distinguished administrative career in the Kalamazoo Public Schools, Debby is now a full-time writer, as is Arnie, who was chairman of the English Department (1997-2007) at Western Michigan University, and taught there for many years as co-founder of the creative writing program and founder of the playwriting program. They are members of the Dramatists Guild, the Associated Writing Programs, Poets & Writers, and the American Literary Translators Association.

Jenny Kalahar is the editor and publisher of *Last Stanza Poetry Journal*. She is the founding leader of Last Stanza Poetry Association  in Elwood, Indiana, now in its tenth year. Jenny and her husband, poet Patrick, are used and rare booksellers. She was the humor columnist for *Tails Magazine* for several years and the treasurer for Poetry Society of Indiana. She is the author of fourteen books; her latest novel series is set in central Indiana. Twice nominated for a Pushcart Prize, her poems have been published in *Tipton Poetry Journal, Indiana Voice Journal, Trillium, Polk Street Review, Flying Island,* and in several anthologies and newspapers. Her works can be found on poemhunter.com and *INverse,* Indiana's poetry archive. She and Patrick previously owned bookshops in Michigan and Ohio. Through her publishing house, Stackfreed Press, she has published books in the US and UK. jennykalahar@att.net

Patrick Kalahar is a used and rare bookseller with his wife, Jenny, and a book conservationist. He is a veteran, world traveler, avid reader, and book collector. He is a member of Last Stanza Poetry Association. His poems have been published in *Tipton* *Poetry Journal, Flying Island, Rail Lines, The Moon and Humans, Polk Street Review, Northwest Indiana Literary Journal,* and *A Disconsolate Planet.*

Chuck Kellum grew up on a farm southwest of Indianapolis. As a young

adult, he traveled to about twenty countries. He eventually settled into a technology-related career primarily as a business applications software developer, married, helped raise three children, and has lived in Anderson, Indiana, since 1984. He began writing poetry while a senior in college studying engineering. He's been a member of the Noble Poets club since 2017, and currently serves as Treasurer and Contest Director of the Poetry Society of Indiana.

Joseph Kerschbaum's most recent publications include *Mirror Box* (Main St Rag Press, 2020) and *Distant Shore of a Split Second* (Louisiana Literature Press, 2018). Joseph has been awarded grants from the National Endowment for the Arts and the Indiana Arts Commission. His work has appeared in journals such as *Poetry Distillery, Hamilton Stone Review, Panoply, Flying Island, Ponder Review,*

Main St. Rag, and *The Delinquent.* Joseph lives in Bloomington, Indiana with his family.

Norbert Krapf, former Indiana Poet Laureate, is a native of Jasper who has published fourteen collections, the latest of which are *Indiana Hill Country Poems* and *Southwest by Midwest.* His *Homecomings* memoir, which covers the fifty years of his writing and publishing life, will be released next year. He has edited, translated, and written a number of books about his German roots, including *Finding the Grain: Pioneer German Germans and Letters, Beneath the Cherry Sapling: Legends from Franconia, Shadows on the Sundial: Early Poems of Rainer Maria Rilke,* and *Blue- Eyed Grass: Poems of Germany.*

His *Looking for God's Country* includes poems inspired by photos of Franconia by Andreas Riedel, whose photos are also included in a collection about Norbert's grandson, *The Return of Sunshine.* Krapf has read many times with Franconian dialect poet and playwright Helmut Haberkamm in Germany and Indiana. They met at the University of Erlangen when Norbert was a Fulbright guest professor of American poetry and Helmut was a Ph.D. candidate in German and English.

Lee Landau produced her first poem at twelve years old, and continues to write poetry, flash fiction and short fiction. Her poems have been published in *Wisconsin Review, Cathexis Northwest, New Millennium Writings,* and *Reed Magazine,* among many others. She has workshopped with Billy Collins, Dara Weir, Tom Lux, Sharon Olds, and Jude Nutter. Lee is a recent transplant from Minnesota to the Gulf shore of Florida where she retired.

Lisa Lewis's most recent books are *The Body Double* (*Georgetown Review* Press) and *Taxonomy of the Missing* (The WordWorks). A chapbook titled *The Borrowing Days* is forthcoming from Emrys Press. Recent work appears or is forthcoming in *Florida Review, Posit, Gulf Coast, Crazyhorse, Interim, Diode, Agni Online,* and elsewhere. She directs the creative writing program at Oklahoma State University and serves as poetry editor for the *Cimarron Review*.

Scott Lowery is a teaching artist and retired educator who splits his time between Rollingtone (MN) and Milwaukee, where he's been lucky to safely weather the pandemic with his wife, granddaughter, son and daughter-in-law, and cats. His collection *Empty-handed* (2013) won the Emergence Poetry Chapbook Award from Red Dragonfly Press, and recent work appears in *Prairie Schooner, Third Wednesday, Naugatuck River Review,* and *Sow's Ear Poetry Review.* Two of his poems are anthologized in *Sheltering with Poems,* a collection of pandemic poems from Bent Paddle Press (2021, Madison WI). Check out "Pandemic Wishes," a group poem from a 2020 Zoom workshop with grade school poets, at scottloweryblog.wordpress.com Scott looks forward to in-person workshops with young poets whenever those opportunities re-emerge.

Deborah Zarka Miller holds an MFA in writing and teaches composition, creative writing, and literature at Anderson University in Indiana. In addition to teaching, she has served as lead grant writer and project manager for several large initiatives funded by Lilly Endowment and is co-director of the university's Honors Program. She was the editor for *The Desk as Altar: The Centennial History of Anderson University,* published in 2016. Her publications include *A Star for Robbins Chapel,* a young adult novella published in 2010 by Chinaberry House, and multiple articles on pedagogy in higher education, all of which appeared in *Faculty Focus.* She also contributed an essay to *Home Again:*

Essays and Memoirs from Indiana, published in 2006 by the *Indiana Historical Society Press.*

A native of South Bend, **John Minczeski** is the author of *A Letter to Serafin* and other collections. Poems appear in past or forthcoming issues of *Harvard Review, The New Yorker, Rhino, Cider Press Review, North Dakota Quarterly*, and elsewhere. He has taught poets in schools and colleges around the Twin Cities.

Lylanne Musselman is an award-winning poet, playwright, and visual artist, living in Indiana. Her work has appeared in *Pank, The New Verse News, Rose Quartz Magazine,* and *The Ekphrastic Review,* among others.  Recently, one of her poems was selected as the featured poem in *Tipton Poetry Journal,* Issue # 48 Spring 2021. Musselman's work has appeared in many anthologies, including *The Indianapolis Anthology* (Belt Publishing, 2021). She is the author of six chapbooks, including *Paparazzi for the Birds* (Red Mare 16, 2018) and is the author of the full-length poetry collection, *It's Not Love, Unfortunately* (Chatter House Press, 2018). Musselman is currently working on several chapbooks and a new manuscript.

James Nolan's latest book of poetry is *Nasty Water: Collected New Orleans Poems* (University of Louisiana at Lafayette Press, 2018).  Previous collections are *Why I Live in the Forest, What Moves Is Not the Wind*, and *Drunk on Salt*, and his translations include volumes of Neruda and Gil de Biedma. His *Flight Risk* won the 2018 Next-Generation Indie Book Award for Best Memoir. The three books of his fiction have been awarded a Faulkner-Wisdom Gold Medal, an Independent Publishers Book Award, and a Next-Generation Indie Book Award. The recipient of an NEA and two Fulbright fellowships, he has taught at universities in San Francisco, Florida, Barcelona, Madrid, Beijing, as well as in his native New Orleans. For more: https://www.pw.org/directory/writers/james_nolan

Thomas Alan Orr has published two collections, *Hammers in the Fog* and *Tongue to the Anvil: New and Selected Poems,* both from Restoration Press in Indianapolis. His poetry has been featured in *Good Poems,* edited by Garrison Keillor, *Growing Season: A Collection of Poems by Midwestern Poets, In Whatever Houses We May Visit: An Anthology of Poems That Have Inspired Physicians, Flying Island, Tipton Poetry Review,* and the *Merton Seasonal.* He is a two-time nominee for the Pushcart Prize.

Joe Ottinger is a retired neurologist from Fort Wayne, Indiana. Growing up near Fishers, Indiana, he lived ten years on a campfire girls camp. He enjoyed the bustle of activity in summers and the quiet solitude along White River the rest of the year. He began writing poetry following retirement in 2014 after forty years in practice.

Rosanne Megenity Peters, a lifelong lover of poetry, lives in Indianapolis where she works as a residential organizer. Reading and writing poetry became lifelines for her during years of accompanying her husband through a difficult illness. After his death, her writing became a vessel, keeping her afloat in the grief. She enjoys gardening, ceramics classes, and musical swings at the new Fort Ben Cultural Campus.

Nancy Kay Peterson's poetry has appeared in print and online in numerous publications, most recently in *HerWords, Lost Lake Folk Opera, One Sentence Poems, Spank the Carp, Steam Ticket, Tipton Poetry Journal* and *Three Line Poetry.* From 2004-2009, she co-edited and co-published *Main Channel Voices: A Dam Fine Literary Magazine* (Winona, MN). Finishing Line Press published her two poetry chapbooks, *Belated Remembrance* and *Selling the Family.* www.nancykaypeterson.com.

William Reichard is a writer, editor, and educator. *Our Delicate Barricades Downed,* his seventh poetry collection, was recently published by Broadstone Books. Previous collections include *The Night Horse: Selected and New Poems* (Brighthorse Books, 2018) and *Two Men Rowing Madly Toward Infinity* (Broadstone Books, 2016).

Stephen R. Roberts has been published in *Alembic, Briar Cliff Review, Borderlands, Willow Springs, Karamu, Water-Stone, Bryant Literary*  *Review, Yalobusha Review, Sulphur River Review, Connecticut River Review, Flying Island*, and many others. He has five published chapbooks including *Rhubarb Desoto* and *Small Fire Speaking in the Rain*. His full-length collection, *Almost Music from Between Places*, is available from Chatter House Press. His newest collection, *Unauthorized Entries and Dim Exits*, still searches for a publisher.

Mary Sexson is author of the award-winning book, *103 in the Light, Selected Poems 1996-2000 (*Restoration Press*)*, co-author of *Company of Women, New and Selected Poems* (Chatter House Press). Her poetry has appeared in *Tipton Poetry Journal, Hoosier Lit, New Verse News*, and several anthologies. Sexson has recent work in *Last Stanza Poetry Journal: Altered States* (Stackfreed Press 2021). Her work is archived in INverse Poetry Archives for Hoosier Poets. Her poetry on the pandemic was published through Indianapolis Writers Center's publication, *What Was and Will Be*. Sexson's poem "Close" was choreographed by Dance Kaleidoscope. Her latest work can be found in *Laureate: Literary Journal of the Arts for Lawrence* (2021).

Christopher Stolle's writing has appeared most recently in *Tipton Poetry Journal, Flying Island, Edify Fiction, Contour, The New Southern Fugitives, The Gambler, Gravel, The Light Ekphrastic, Sheepshead Review*, and *Plath Poetry Project*. He's an editor for DK Publishing, and he lives in Richmond, Indiana.

Paris Tate is the author of *All the Words in Between*. Her poetry can also be found in the anthology *Maple Leaf Rag*, literary journals such as *Tilted House Review*, *The New Guard Review*, and *Infection House*, a New Orleans-based online literary magazine that focused on life during the COVID-19 pandemic and other events that defined 2020. Born and raised in a suburb just outside of New Orleans, Louisiana, Tate continues to live near New Orleans where she works in a library and will be attaining her Master's in Library and Information Science from Louisiana State University.

Diana Thoresen is a Russian-Australian writer, photographer and independent publisher currently residing in Palm Cove, North Queensland. She's interested in free energy research and translating rare texts about anti-gravity experiments.

Rp Verlaine lives in New York City. He has an MFA in creative writing from City College. He taught in New York Public schools for many years. His first volume of poetry, *Damaged by Dames & Drinking,* was published in 2017, and *Femme Fatales, Movie Starlets & Rockers* in 2018. A set of three e-books began with the publication of *Lies from The Autobiography, Vol 1,* in November of 2018. Vol 2 was published in 2019, and the third in 2020. A new collection, *Far Too Close and Further,* awaits publication in 2021. His poetry has appeared in *Atlas Poetica, The Linnet's Wings, Moving Images, Scissortail Quarterly, Chrysanthemum Literary Anthology, Last Stanza Poetry Journal, Dear Booze Cocktails, Wales Haiku Journal The Mainichi, Splintered Disorder Press, Rigorous, The South Shore Review, The Local Train, Proletaria, Haikuniverse, Scry of Lust 2* anthology, *Rudderless Mariner, Humankind Journal, The Wild Word, Under The Basho, Plum Tree Tavern, Fresh Out Magazine, Scissortail Quarterly, Prune Juice, Incense Dreams, Last Leaves, Blazevox, Pikers Press, Poems 'bout Love & Hate* anthology, *Stardust Haiku,* and *Heart of Flesh.*

Melody Wang currently resides in sunny Southern California with her dear husband. In her free time, she dabbles in piano composition. She enjoys hiking, baking, and playing with her dogs. She can be found on Twitter @MelodyOfMusings

James Eric Watkins creates from and often resides on the far side of sanity. He is guided by benevolence and sees beauty and pain side by side in a balance of love, a balance which manifests into the artistic expression that allows him to exist in this world.

Rita Yager is a nurse/teacher/photographer who writes about marginalized, at risk, and special needs populations. Poetry is her vehicle for delivering words about things that most people are afraid to admit that they feel, hopes her words give a voice that offers comfort and inclusion. She's been writing for fifty years, but only began submitting poetry after age sixty-five. She loves to write about relationships, nature, whimsy, and children.

Hiromi Yoshida was a finalist for the 2019 New Women's Voices Poetry Prize for *Icarus Burning* (Finishing Line Press, 2020).  She is a freelance writer and editor who serves as a poetry reader for *Flying Island* and as a diversity consultant for the Writers Guild at Bloomington. She is a copyeditor for *Gidra* and leads a poetry workshop for the award-winning VITAL program at the Monroe County Public Library. Her poems have been nominated for inclusion in the Sundress Best of the Net anthology and have been added to the INverse Poetry Archive. She enjoys contemplating the oddities of life, such as abandoned houses, wildflowers blooming from gravel, and birdsong in thunderstorm.

Made in the USA
Monee, IL
18 July 2021